LALJAY KOLKATA
14/02/2016

PAÑCHĪKARAṆAM

Text and the Varttika with word-for-word Translation, English Rendering, Comments and Glossary

D0672789

Advaita Ashrama
(PUBLICATION DEPARTMENT)
5 DEHI ENTALLY ROAD • KOLKATA 700 014

Published by
Swami Tattwavidananda
Adhyaksha, Advaita Ashrama
Mayavati, Champawat, Uttarakhand, Himalayas
from its Publication Department, Kolkata
Email : mail@advaitaashrama.org
Website : www.advaitaashrama.org

© *All Rights Reserved*
Eleventh Reprint, December 2013
1M1C

ISBN 978-81-7505-108-9

Printed in India at
Trio Process
Kolkata 700 014

PREFACE TO THE SECOND EDITION

This English translation of the valuable treatise on Vedānta, *Pañcīkaraṇam* of Śrī Śaṅkarācārya with *Vārttika* of Śrī Sureśvarācārya, was first published by the Ramakrishna Mission Sevashrama, Vrindaban, in 1962. The book has been out of print for quite a while. At the request of the original publisher we are now publishing it in its present form.

We hope all lovers of Vedānta will welcome its re-publication.

ADVAITA ASHRAMA
MAYAVATI ALMORA HIMALAYAS
September 29, 1971

PUBLISHER

PREFACE TO THE FIRST EDITION

It is a pleasure for us to place before the public Śrī Śaṅkara's "*Pañcīkaraṇam*" with Śrī Sureśvara's *Vārttika* on it, both translated into English with suitable explanatory notes, wherever considered necessary.

Characterised by extreme brevity of expression on the one hand and marvellous sublimity of thought on the other, this work of Śrī Śaṅkara contains the quintessence of the Upaniṣads. Its subject-matter is the same as that of the *Māṇḍūkya Upaniṣad*, presenting as it does, the theoretical aspect of the One Reality and the practical way of realizing one's identity with It in *Samādhi* through the help of the time-honoured symbol, AUM.

The object of a *Vārttika* is three-fold, viz (1) to explain what has been said, (2) to mention what has been omitted, and (3) to point out what has been imperfectly stated in the original text. Śrī Sureśvara, famous for his monumental *Vārttikas* on Śrī Śaṅkara's commentaries on the *Bṛhadāraṇyaka* and *Taittirīya Upaniṣads*, has written a *Vārttika* on this small treatise, consisting of 64 *ślokas* elucidating and amplifying the ideas contained in the original text.

This book is dedicated to the loving and revered memory of Srimat Swami Jagadanandaji Maharaj of the Ramakrishna Order, who passed away at the Ramakrishna Mission Sevasrama, Vrindaban, in December, 1951. Himself fully convinced of the standpoint of Śrī Śaṅkara's philosophy, he taught and preached almost to the last day of his life the message of Advaita. In fact, he used to recommend these two works of the great Teachers to beginners for the study of Vedānta. It is, therefore, a matter of no small satisfaction for us, that we have been able to dedicate this book to his sacred memory.

We hope that the translation, explanatory notes, the glossary of important terms and the Introduction will be of use to English-knowing people—spiritual aspirants, inclined to the path of Knowledge, as well as those who are interested in an intellectual understanding of this aspect of Indian Philosophy and *sādhanā*.

Many have helped us in diverse ways in the publication of this book. We take this opportunity to express our heartfelt thanks to all of them. We are especially grateful to Swami Hiranmayananda, Head of the Ramakrishna Mission Vidyapith at Deoghar and Purulia, for his nice Foreword and to Sri S. S. Raghavachar, M.A., of the Mysore University for having favoured us with a most valuable Introduction to the *Pañcīkaraṇam* and the *Pañcīkaraṇa-Vārttikam.*

RAMAKRISHNA MISSION SEVASHRAMA PUBLISHER
VRINDABAN DT. MATHURA U.P.
January 28, 1962

FOREWORD

The *Pañcīkaraṇam* is a small treatise on the Advaita philosophy by Śrī Śaṅkarācārya. It is a *Prakaraṇa* work, i.e. a topical discussion dealing with one or more moot points, as distinguished from the consideration of the subject-matter in its entirety. It is not necessary to dilate here on the life and teachings of Śrī Śaṅkara. His is the greatest name in Indian philosophy. Since his time philosophy has meant either refutation or elucidation and ratification of his position.

According to the Advaita standpoint only Brahman is real and all else is unreal. This unreality of the world, however, does not signify total negation. The world exists as an empirical necessity but not as a transcendental validity. As an illusory experience is sublated by the empirical knowledge, so is empirical knowledge sublated by the higher transcendental knowledge. Epistomologically, in an experience two things are involved, I and You, the subject and the object. These two are completely distinct and different as regards contents and qualities. But even then they are somehow mixed up and identified in the process of experience. Why this is so cannot be explained. But the practice is natural with people—"नैसर्गिकोऽयं लोकव्यवहारः". (Br. Sū. Adhyāsa Bhāṣya). Or, as Swami Vivekananda puts it : 'It is a statement of facts.' Logically, however, the question how the absolute

Brahman, came to be manifested as the relative world cannot be posed at all. The absolute is beyond the scope of any logical formulation.

Nevertheless, ontological enquiry leads us to the determination of the primal cause of the fact of our experience which the world is. And the theory of *Pañcīkaraṇam* is adduced in explanation of the origination of the world from the one Reality that exists, Brahman. Brahman transforms Itself serially into the five rudimentary elements which, by admixture in different proportions, create the phenomenal world. Brahman, thus, is both the efficient as well as the material cause of the world. But this is only apparently. Really there is neither transformation nor the world. This is the well-known *Vivartavāda*, according to which the transformation is not real but due to imaginary attribution (*Adhyāsa*) only. The Jīva or the individual soul in such a background is illusory. His real nature is the same as that of Brahman. It is through ignorance that he considers himself limited and sees the diversity in the world.

In the light of the above discussion we have to understand the phenomenal world. This world exists as a fact of experience. And this experience flows as three streams of consciousness—the waking, the dream and the deep-sleep—the gross, the subtle and the causal states. By an analysis of these three states can we arrive at a proper explanation of the world-phenomena. Transcending these three states and encompassing them is the fourth state—Brahman. This in fact is no state at all, being beyond all perception. This is called a state in order to fit it into the serial order of the above three. And this matter has been very succinctly and clearly expounded by Śrī Śaṅkara in *Pañcīkaraṇam.*

There is also another topic which has been elaborated in this work : the significance of the syllable 'AUM' and its correlation to the world. This world according to the Vedanta Philosophy is a composite of name and form. It is shown in this book how the different letters of the syllable 'AUM' stand for the names of the gross, the subtle and the causal states of the world. 'A' stands for the gross, 'U' for the subtle, 'M' for the causal, and the syllable 'AUM' for the transcendental.

The aim of this work, however, is not merely the satisfaction of scholastic interest regarding ontological problems, but to lead people through such discussions to the realization of the Ultimate Reality. In this realization alone lies the salvation from the sufferings and miseries of the world.

The faith in the reality of the phenomenal world is so deep-rooted in our minds that it is very difficult to get rid of it and attain to the knowledge of the Ultimate Reality. One of the methods by which this can be achieved is by *Upāsanā*. By *Upāsanā* is meant by Śaṅkara, "the process of taking hold of some stay or *ālambana*', established as such in the Śāstras and directing a continuous flow of even psychoses towards it, without the intervention of any other cognitions contrary to it." (Chāndogya Up., Śaṅkara's interpretation, 1. i. 1).

Many such stay or '*ālambanas*' have been prescribed by the Scriptures. But the most sacred and ancient of them is 'AUM'. It has been said in the *Kaṭha Upaniṣad* :

एतदालम्बनं श्रेष्ठमेतदालम्बनं परम् ।
एतदालम्बनं ज्ञात्वा ब्रह्मलोके महीयते ॥ (1.2.17)

"This 'stay' is the best and this 'stay' is the highest. By knowing this 'stay' one becomes great in the *Brahamaloka*". And in this book the method of *Upāsanā* by 'AUM' has been elaborately presented.

The importance of the work can be realized from the fact that even the great Sureśvarācārya has thought it worthwhile to write a commentary on this small brochure. As a work which gives the quintessence of the Vedāntic theory, and withal, delineates pointedly and authoritatively, how his theory can be realized in life, surely this commands the attention of all students of Vedānta. The English translation seeks to make this important work available to those who have no knowledge of Sanskrit or whose knowledge of Sanskrit is too inadequate to allow the study of this book in the original.

SWAMI HIRANMAYANANDA

INTRODUCTION

The Pañcīkaraṇam and the Pañcīkaraṇa-Vārttikam

Concerning the Original :

Pañcīkaraṇam is one of the shortest of the minor works attributed to Śrī Śaṅkarācārya. Usually, in the printed editions there is a spurious opening paragraph added to the text:

अथातः परमहंसानां समाधिविधिं व्याख्यास्यामः ।
................निष्प्रपंचं प्रपञ्च्यते ॥

That this did not form a part of the original is evidenced by the silence of the standard commentaries on it. The remaining part, coherent and fairly complete, opens with the words "*Pañcīkṛta*", and that perhaps is responsible for the title of the work which, is not quite indicative of its theme. The very popular Advaita manual *Pañcadaśī* alludes to it once as '*Pañcīkaraṇam*' thus assigning to it an authoritative status and also authenticating its traditional title (9th Chapter, 64th Verse). His Holiness Śrī Śaṅkarācārya of Kāmakoṭipīṭham has sanctioned its publication as a genuine work of Śaṅkara. These and the existence of several commentaries from well-known writers go a long way in showing the attitude of the Advaita tradition towards it and also the title under which it has come down.

Though the work is very short, it deals with the fundamental theme of Advaita. It distinguishes the Ātman from its empirical adjunct. It analyses the adjunct into three bodies, causal, subtle and gross. It defines the three states of waking, dream and deep-sleep. It points to the absolute unity and divinity of Ātman in its intrinsic reality as transcending the three-fold adjunct. Contemplation of this final truth through the sacred symbol "AUM", highly glorified in the entire Hindu tradition, is inculcated in the text. The work is designed to propound the fundamental philosophy of Advaita and formulate a method of inward con emplation productive of final spiritual realization. It is this specific nature of the text that is taken in *Pañcadaśī* as authorising the *upāsanā* on *Nirguṇa* Brahman. There is one other text of greater antiquity and authority working out the same theme—that is the *Māṇḍūkya Upaniṣad*. The present work seems to be consciously modelled on that Upaniṣad and *Pañcadaśī* notes the affinity of the two works. It says:

> माण्डुक्यादौ च सर्वत्र निर्गुणोपास्तिरीरिता ।
> अनुष्ठानप्रकारोऽस्याः पञ्चीकरण ईरितः ।। पञ्चदशी---९।६३,६४

The *Vārttika* of Śrī Sureśvara also specifies this object of the treatise in its first verse :

The syllable "AUM" is the essence of the Vedas and it is revelatory of ultimate reality. The method of contemplation through that fundamental and significant symbol is presented herein for practice by the aspirants after liberation.

Concerning the Vārttika :

Vārttika is a commentary that supplements, elaborates and critically restates the thesis of the original. In the Advaitic tradition Śrī Sureśvara is the *Vārttikakāra*. He has written this type of commentary on Śaṅkara's Bhāṣyas on the *Taittirīya* and *Bṛhadāraṇyaka Upaniṣads.* A work called *Mānasollāsa* is a *vārttika* accepted by tradition as a composition by Sureśvara on the Hymns addressed to *Dakṣiṇāmūrty* ascribed to Śaṅkara. *Naiṣkarmya-Siddhi* is an important and independent treatise of Sureśvara. The present work elucidating and elaborating the *Pañcīkaraṇam* of Śaṅkara is attributed to Sureśvara. While usually it is named *Pañcīkaraṇa-Vārttikam*, Sri Mahadeva Sastry, in his Adyar edition, calls it *Praṇava-Vārttikam.* The latter title is fine and does suit the theme of the treatise eminently. But Sri Mahadeva Sastry does not state the authority for his choice of title.

The Substance of the Vārttika :

Following the *Māṇḍūkya Upaniṣad* and *Pañcīkaraṇam*, the *Vārttika* offers a brief statement of the philosophy of Advaita. This it does in the course of sixty-four felicitous verses. It follows what may be described as the dogmatic style and it contains no discussions or arguments. The style fits the character of the work designed as a direction to contemplation. The matter presented briefly is of utmost significance and we may attempt an analysis of it :

(*a*) Human experience passes through three states, waking, dream and deep-sleep. These three must be studied closely and their distinctive characteristics noted. In waking there is the experience of the solid external world through sense-perception. In dream senses do not function. The impressions deposited in the mind by previous experiences are revivified and shaped into the likeness of waking itself. The internal perception by the mind of these revivified impressions lodged within itself, as if they are realities of the waking state itself, is dream. In deep-sleep neither the senses nor the mind functions. The self withdraws into itself as it were, but there is no self-understanding. The self is covered by a primeval ignorance, from which spring all wakings, and dreams. This ignorance covers the self in all its states, but it does not set up the presentation of the non-self in the deep-sleep as it does in waking and dream.

(*b*) This analysis of the states brings out the three-fold nature of embodiment. In the waking state the self is embodied in what is called the gross body consisting of the five gross elements and their modifications. The theory which gives the title to the work concerns the gross elements. In the Vedic philosophy of nature, at least three stages are discernible. In the first stage, as represented by the *Chāndogya Upaniṣad*, three elements, namely, Fire, Water and Earth are posited. In the second stage, as represented, for instance, in the *Taittirīya Upaniṣad*, there is the addition of Air and Ethereal space. Further on, the empirical fact that these elements are not to be found in their pure and unmixed state and that they are clearly independent substances is not much of a demonstrated scientific truth must have led to the explanation that the five elements are pure and independent only in their subtle state, while as found empirically they are mixed up a great deal. Each empirically given gross element has within it, according to this view, all the other elements also. For instance in the gross Earth, half of it consists of pure earth and the other half consists of the other four pure elements. This process of the composition of the gross elements is what is called *Pañcīkarṇam*. Experience of these elements and their products through sense-perception is characteristic of waking life. In the dream-state the embodiment is said to be subtle. The body of the dream-self, in the first place, contains organs of knowledge and organs of action, which are ten in all and are called *Indriyas*. It also contains the five vital breaths called *Prāṇas*. It has the internal sense, (*Antaḥkaraṇa*) consisting of intellect (*Buddhi*), mind (*Manas*), the Ego-sense (*Ahaṁkāra*) and the faculty of contemplation (*Citta*). It also contains the five subtle elements. In addition to these five factors, i.e. organs of knowledge, organs of action, vital breath, internal sense and the subtle elements, it also has their foundation *Avidyā*, *Kāma* and *Karma*. These eight factors, according to the *Vārttika*, constitute the subtle body of the self. According to another enumeration, the subtle body consists of seventeen factors. They are the ten organs of knowledge and action, the five vital breaths, the intellect and the mind. This is the analysis of the subtle body as decisively given in some works like *Saṅksepa Śārīraka* (3-20).

The *Pañcīkaraṇa* itself enumerates the five subtle elements, the five breaths, the ten *Indriyas*, *Manas* and *Buddhi* as constituting the seventeen-fold subtle body. The numbering of the factors here is quite unintelligible if we include the subtle elements. The *Vārttika* describes the subtle body as the eight-fold fortress and gives the first enumeration of factors. There is a difficulty here and perhaps the solution of the *Saṅkṣepa Śārīraka* is the right one. Any way there is a clear enough divergence here between the original and the *Vārttika*. In deep-sleep the body of the self is said to be causal, meaning that it is the seed of the subtle and gross bodies and that it is the pure unactualized potentiality of the body. It consists of the original Nescience from which spring the phenomenal manifestations of the dream and waking worlds. This Nescience is not the negation of the native consciousness of the Ātman, for it must itself subsist in the presence of that consciousness, even as a cloud, however much it may conceal the Sun, owes its being to the Sun. Moreover, it covers and does not annihilate the self-effulgence of the Ātman. This Nescience truly defies definition, analysis and description. It is neither real nor unreal. Nor is it both real and unreal. It is neither one nor many, nor one and many. It is neither simple nor composite, nor both. All that can be positively asserted about it is that it is subject to termination by only the knowledge of the identity of Brahman and Ātman. The problem of explaining it does not arise when one is unaware of the Ātman. When he comes to be aware of the Ātman, the ignorance has disappeared and does not exist enough to call for an explanation. It is only the co-existence of the clear awareness of the Ātman and ignorance concerning it that would raise a problem. But that co-existence is impossible. Hence the nature of the primeval Nescience is inexplicable. But it positively disappears when we awake to reality. This ignorance is the causal body operating by itself in the state of deep-sleep. Thus the Ātman is encased in a threefold body.

(*c*) The three states and the three bodies are relative to the self. We can speak of three selves from the empirical standpoint in relation to the states and bodies. The self as embodied in the gross body and undergoing the experiences of waking is called *Viśva.* The self as encased in the subtle body and undergoing dream-experiences is the *Taijasa.* The self as resting in the causal body in the state of deep-sleep is the *Prājña.* This is the terminology to be adopted when we take an individualistic or Microcosmic point of view. But if we adopt the Macrocosmic point of view and regard the totality of being, the Cosmic Self or Deity can be said to maintain itself in three planes of phenomenal manifestation. In its primordial plane as associated with Māyā or cosmic self-concealment it is *Akṣara.* As enfolded in the cosmic totality of subtle bodies and dream-state, it is *Sūtrātman* or *Hiraṇyagarbha.* In relation to the totality of the gross universe as revealed to waking consciousness, the cosmic spirit is said to be *Virāṭ.* Thus there are three phases of the individual self corresponding to the three planes of the phenomenal appearance of the universal spirit.

(*d*) *Praṇava* or the Syllable 'AUM' consists of three component elements. They are A, U and M.

The *Māṇḍūkya Upaniṣad* initiated the tradition of regarding the three sound elements of *Aum* as corresponding to and as signifying the phases of the self conditioned by the three bodies, and as manifesting itself in the three phenomenal states. *Pañcīkaraṇa* follows it closely. The *Vārttika* elaborates this theory of correspondence between the sound-elements and the planes of the spirit's phenomenal manifestation. The theory rescues the syllable *Aum* from the realm of the meaningless and the Occult and invests it with supreme import and converts it into a vehicle of the highest Vedāntic truth. We are told that 'A' signifies the *Virāṭ* in the Macrocosm and the *Viśva* in the Microcosm. 'U' is said to represent *Taijasa* and *Hiraṇyagarbha*. 'M' is taken as signifying *Prājña* and *Īśvara*. While this correspondence is inculcated, the devotee is asked to dismiss the difference between the Microcosm and the Macrocosm and to apprehend as one and identical *Viśva* and *Virāṭ*, *Taijasa* and *Hiraṇyagarbha*. and *Prājña* and *Īśvara*. This fusion of the particular and cosmic standpoints is insisted upon and we are to see in the three constituents of *Aum* the signification of the three phases of the one integral spirit.

(*e*) Thus the whole universe is viewed in three levels, the causal, the subtle and the gross. The spirit which is the ultimate reality, appears conditioned by these. Now the philosophical problem for man is to ascend to the apprehension of the real as transcending the conditions in which it is seemingly embodied. The spiritual problem is to release oneself from these limiting conditions and to realize one's identity with

2

the ultimate principle. The symbol *Aum* is maintained to contain the direction for developing this transcendent integrality of knowledge and life. The first sound-constituent of *Aum,* namely 'A' represents the gross point of view. It connotes the naive realism and pluralism of common sense. From this we ought to move on to the level of thought represented by 'U'. 'U' signifies the understanding of the world as the projection of the universe by the Spirit itself. The point of view is found on the dream-experience and its philosophy may be described as Dynamic Idealism. Spirit, through the instrumentality of mind, sets up within itself the entire cosmos. When this standpoint reaches maturity, we must pass beyond it The next stage is represented by 'M'. The diversity of presentation conjured up in the dream-world is nothing real. It is a projection of the unreal. Such projection is founded upon the non-apprehension of the real. The realization of this fact of radical non-apprehension is promoted by the consideration of the experience of deep-sleep. We dream because we are asleep. The world taken as real in waking is really of the same status as dream-world and the pre-supposition of such cosmic dreaming is the failure to see that the Ātman is the sole reality. This failure is most clearly illustrated in deep-sleep. We must pass into the frame of thought according to which our empirical life which is in reality a dream is due to our being asleep to spirit, the fundamental substance of our being. We are most asleep when we fancy ourselves most awake. Even as the chanting of the sacred *Praṇava* culiminates in the serenity of silence after the final sound 'M', the philosophic contemplation of man's experience in its entirety must pass after the consideration of the state of deep-sleep into the unconditioned effulgence of the pure and transcendent Self. The seed of phenomenal life namely ignorance most strikingly present in sleep must be destroyed and the sleeper must wake up to the infinite reality of his spiritual essence. This ultimate self-affirmation is the goal of contemplation. The agnosticism of sleep must be burnt up in this transcendent self-realization. Following the *Praṇava* in all its phases, and to its farthest merger in silence, one must review the spirit's manifestation in the three states and upto its embodiment in the Nescience-body and pass beyond even that causal sheath into the utter freedom of its absolute illumination. An analysis of man's three states does thus fulfil itself in the vision of his Divine essence in all the glory of its "stateless" eternity.

(*f*) The *Pañcīkaraṇa-Vārttika* advises the spiritual aspirant to practise meditation on this theme with zest and devotion and promises as a result the final emancipation from all bondage.

A word may be said concerning the place of meditation in the spiritual discipline formulated in Advaita Vedānta. Knowledge is the liberating factor. When knowledge is mediate and is still of the nature of the simple understanding of *Mahā-Vākyas* aided by human reason, some part of the basic ignorance constitutive of bondage gets destroyed. When this mediate understanding transforms itself into direct and immediate realization, it destroys the remaining portion of ignorance. Even after this realization the embodiment of the self may not cease and does continue as long as the *Prārabdha Karma* remains inexhausted. This stage is called *Jīvan-Mukti.* When *Prārabdha* is liquidated liberation in the completest sense gets achieved. The first stage of knowledge is rendered possible by Karma-Yoga in the spirit of the Gītā and the four spiritual acquisitions called *Sādhana-catuṣṭaya.* The mediate realization of Vedāntic truth is converted into immediate realization by meditation of the type described in our treatise. The liquidation of *Prārabdha* is effected in the natural course determined by the law of Karma. Thus meditation is destructive of the hindrances to the transformation of mediate philosophical knowledge into direct spiritual realization. Śrī Śaṅkara's *Pañcīkaraṇam* and the *Vārttika* on it by Śrī Sureśvara are designed to set forth the pattern of this meditation. It is a wholly praiseworthy achievement to have made the *Praṇava* the focus of this meditation. It is an equally remarkable contribution to have read into the *Praṇava* the entire philosophy of Advaita Vedānta.

S. S. Raghavachar, M. A.
Department of Philosophy,
University of Mysore

BROAD ANALYSIS
OF
THE 'VĀRTTIKA'

1. Descent from the Pure Brahman to *Virāṭ*

   Verses: 1 to 11

2. The description of the three bodies, three states and the identification of the threefold microcosm with the threefold macrocosm.

   Verses: 12 to 45

3. Fusion of *Aum* with the three states and the process of gradual resolution of all into the Ātman.

   Verses: 46 to 52

4. The grand description of the final liberation or Pure Brahman.

   Verses: 53 to 64

LIST OF ABBREVIATIONS

Upaniṣads :

Ai.	..	..	Aitareya
Bṛ.	..	..	Bṛhadāraṇyaka
Chā.	..	..	Chāndogya
Ka.	..	..	Kaṭha
Mā.	..	..	Māṇḍūkya
Mu.	..	..	Muṇḍaka
Nṛ.Pū.	..	..	Nṛsiṁha-Pūrva-Tāpanī
Subāl.	..	..	Subāla
Śv.	..	..	Śvetāśvatara
Tai.	..	..	Taittirīya

Other works :

Br. Sū.	..	..	Brahma-Sūtras
Bṛ. Vār	..	..	Bṛhadāraṇyaka-Vārttika
Gī.	..	..	Bhagavad-Gītā
Nai.Si.	..	..	Naiṣkarmya-Siddhi
Pañc.	..	..	Pañcadaśī
Up.Sāh.	..	..	Upadeśa-Sāhasrī
Vā.Vṛ.	..	..	Vākya-Vṛtti
Viv. Cū.	..	..	Viveka-Cūḍāmaṇi
Yo.Sū.	..	..	Yoga-Sūtras

ॐ

श्रीमच्छंकराचार्यविरचितम्

पञ्चीकरणम्

PAÑCIKARAṆAM

A small treatise on Vedānta

by Bhagavān Śrī Śaṅkarācārya

ॐ पञ्चीकृतपञ्चमहाभूतानि तत्कार्यं च सर्वं विराडित्युच्यते । एतत्स्थूलशरीरमात्मनः । इन्द्रियैरर्थोपलब्धिर्जागरितम् । तदुभयाभिमान्यात्मा विश्वः । एतत् त्रयमकारः ॥

ॐ *Aum* विराट् इति *Virāṭ*, उच्यते is said, to be the aggregate of सर्वं all, the पञ्चीकृत-पञ्च-महाभूतानि quintuplicated five elements, च and, तत्कार्यं their effects. एतत् This, is the स्थूलशरीरम् gross body, आत्मनः of the Ātman. जागरितम् Waking, is that state, where इन्द्रियैः the senses, अर्थ-उपलब्धिः give rise to the knowledge of objects. आत्मा The Ātman, अभिमानी who has the sense of ownership, in relation to तत् उभय—both the waking state and the gross body, is called विश्वः the *Viśva*. एतत् These त्रयम् three, together are represented by अकारः the first letter 'A' in '*Aum*'.

AUM. The *Virāṭ* is said to be the sum total of all the quintuplicated[1] five elements and their effects. This is called the gross body of the Ātman. Waking[2] is that state, where the senses give rise to the knowledge of objects. The Ātman which identifies Itself with both the waking state and the gross body is known as the '*Viśva*'[3]. These three[4] (the gross body, the waking state and the *Viśva*) together are represented by the first letter 'A' in the syllable '*Aum*'.

1 *Quintuplicated*—A particular process by which the five elementary constituents of the universe are said to be compounded with one another to form grosser entities that serve as units in the composition of the physical universe. For details see verses 7 to 11 of the *Vārttika*.
2 *Waking*—See verses 13 to 29.
3 *Viśva*—See verse 30.
4 *These three*—See verses 45 to 47.

अपञ्चीकृतपञ्चमहाभूतानि पञ्चतन्मात्राणि, तत्कार्यं च पञ्च प्राणाः, दशेन्द्रियाणि, मनोबुद्धिश्चेति सप्तदशकं लिंगम् भौतिकं हिरण्यगर्भं इत्युच्यते। एतत्सूक्ष्मशरीरमात्मनः।

पञ्च-तन्मात्राणि The rudimentary elements, i.e. अपञ्चीकृत-पञ्च-महा-भूतानि the five elements before going through the process of quintuplication or five-fold combination च and तत्कार्यं their effects, भौतिकं the material, लिङ्गम् subtle body, सप्तदशकं having seventeen parts—viz पञ्च the five प्राणाः vital forces दश-इन्द्रियाणि the ten organs of perception and action, मनः the mind, बुद्धिः च इति and the intellect, are together उच्यते called हिरण्यगर्भं इति the *Hiranyagarbha*. एतत् This is said to be the सुक्ष्मशरीरम् subtle body, आत्मनः of the Ātman.

The five unquintuplicated rudimentary elements and their effect, the subtle body, both together constitute what is called the '*Hiranyagarbha*'.[1] The material subtle body has seventeen parts, viz the five

1 *The Hiranyagarbha*—See verses 31-39 and verse 6, note 2.

vital forces, the ten organs of perception and action, the mind and the intellect. This is said to be the subtle body of the Ātman.

करणेषूपसंहृतेषु जागरितसंस्कारजः प्रत्ययः सविषयः स्वप्न इत्युच्यते। तदुभयाभिमान्यात्मा तैजसः। एतत् त्रयमुकारः।

करणेषु उपसंहृतेषु When the sense-organs are quiescent, प्रत्ययः the knowledge, जागरित-संस्कारजः arising from impressions of the waking state, सविषयः along with its imaginary objects, उच्यते is called, स्वप्न इति the dream state. आत्मा The Ātman, तत्-उभय-अभिमानी which identifies Itself with both the dream state and the subtle body, is called तैजसः *Taijasa.* त्रयम् These, त्रयम three—the subtle body, the dream state and the '*Taijasa*' are represented by उकारः the second letter 'U' in '*Aum*'.

When the sense-organs are quiescent or withdrawn, the knowledge arising out of impressions of the waking state and the imaginary objects there perceived, are together called the dream state. The '*Taijasa*'[1] is the Ātman which identifies Itself with both the dream state and the subtle body. These three, i.e.—the subtle body, the dream state and the '*Taijasa*'—are represented by the second letter 'U' in '*Aum*'.

1 The *Taijasa*—see verse 39.

शरीरद्वयकारणमात्माज्ञानं साभासमव्याकृतमित्युच्यते। एतत् कारणशरीरमात्मनः। तच्च न सन्नासन्नापि सदसन्न भिन्नं नाभिन्नं नापि भिन्नाभिन्नं कुतश्चित्, न निरवयवं, न सावयवं नोभयं, किंतु केवलब्रह्मात्मैकत्वज्ञानापनोद्यम्।

साभासम् Connected with the reflection of Pure Consciousness, आत्मा-अज्ञानं the Nescience of the Ātman, शरीर-द्वय-कारणम् which is the cause of both the gross and subtle bodies उच्यते is called अव्याकृतम् इति the -*'Avyākarta'* or undifferentiated. एतत् This, is the कारणशरीरम् causal body आत्मनः of the Ātman. तत् च This is, neither, सत् existent, न असत् nor non-existent, न अपि सत् असत् nor even both existent and non-existent; न भिन्नं neither different from न अभिन्नं nor identical with, न भिन्न-अभिन्नं nor both different from and identical with कुतः चित् anything (i.e., the Ātman). This Nescience is न निरवयवं neither non-composite, न सावयवं nor composite, न उभयं nor both composite and non-composite, किंतु but केवल-ब्रह्म-आत्मा-एकत्व-ज्ञान-अपनोद्यम् removable by the knowledge of the identity of Brahman and the Ātman alone.

Bound up with the reflection of Pure-consciousness, the Nescience,[1] which hides the Ātman and is the cause of both the gross and subtle bodies, is called the *'Avyākṛta'* or undifferentiated. This is the causal body of the Ātman. This is neither existent, nor non-existent, nor even both existent and non-existent; neither different from, nor identical with, nor both different from and identical with, the Ātman. This Nescience is neither composite, nor noncomposite, nor both composite and non-composite, but removable by the knowledge of the identity of Brahman and the Ātman alone.

1. *Nescience or Māyā*—See verses 39-41 and see verse 2, note 4.

सर्वप्रकारज्ञानोपसंहारे बुद्धेः कारणात्मनाऽवस्थानं सुषुप्तिः। तदुभयाभिमान्यात्मा प्राज्ञः। एतत् त्रयम् मकारः॥

सर्व-प्रकार-ज्ञान-उपसंहारे When all thoughts of the waking and dream states are withdrawn, and बुद्धेः the intellect, कारणात्मना अवस्थानं merges into its causal condition, it is called सुषुप्तिः the deep-sleep state. आत्मा The Ātman, तत्-उभय-अभिमानी which identifies Itself with these two, i.e., the deep-sleep state and the causal-body Nescience, is described as प्राज्ञः *Prājña.* एतत् These, त्रयम् three, i.e.—the causal-body Nescience, the deep-sleep state and the *prājña*, are symbolised by मकारः the last letter 'M' in '*Aum*'.

When all thoughts cease and the determinative intellect too, lapses into its causal condition, the state of deep-sleep[1] appears. The personality appropriating these two, i.e., the causal-body and the deep-sleep state is described as, '*Prājña*'[2].

These three (the causal-body Nescience, the deep-sleep state and the '*Prājña*') are symbolised by the last letter 'M' in '*Aum*'.

1 *Deep-sleep*—See verse 42.
2 *Prāna*—See verse 43.
3 *Letter 'M'*—See verse 47.

अकार उकारे, उकारो मकारे, मकार ओंकारे, ओंकारोऽहम्येव। अहमात्मा साक्षी केवलश्चिन्मात्रस्वरूपः, नाज्ञानं नापि तत्कार्यं किंतु नित्यशुद्धबुद्धमुक्तसत्यस्वभावं परमानन्दाद्वयं प्रत्यग्भूतचैतन्यं ब्रह्मैवाहमस्मीत्यभेदेनावस्थानं समाधिः।

Now अकारः the letter 'A' in *Aum*, should be

resolved उकारे into 'U'—i.e., the waking-personality '*Viśva*', symbolised by 'A', should be merged in the dream-personality '*Taijasa*' symbolised by 'U', and उकार: the dream-personality symbolised by 'U' should be resolved मकारे into the deep-sleep-personality symbolised by 'M'. Again मकार: the deep-sleep-personality should be merged ओंकारे into AUM and lastly ओंकार: the AUM अहमि एव in 'I'. अहम् I am, आत्मा the Ātman, साक्षी the Witness of all, केवल: the Absolute and चित्-मात्र-स्वरूप: of the nature of Pure Consciousness, I am न अज्ञानं neither Nescience, न अपि nor even, तत् कार्यं its effect, किंतु but, अहम् I, अस्मि am ब्रह्म एव Brahman alone, नित्य-शुद्ध-बुद्ध-मुक्त-सत्य-स्वभावं Eternally Pure, Ever Enlightened, Eternally Free and Existence Absolute. I am the परम-आनंद Bliss absolute, अद्वयं One without a second and the प्रत्यक्-भूत-चैतन्यं Innermost Consciousness. इति अभेदेन अवस्थानं Thus remaining in unity without any trace of difference is what is called समाधि: '*Samādhi*' or the Superconscious state.

Now, 'A' the waking-personality, should[1] be resolved into 'U', the dream-personality, and the 'U' into 'M' i.e., the deep-sleep personality. Again the 'M' should be reduced into '*Aum*' and the '*Aum*' into 'I'. I am, the Ātman, the Witness of all, the absolute, of the nature of Pure Consciousness; I am neither Nescience nor even its effect but I am Brahman alone, Eternally Pure, Ever Enlightened, Eternally Free and Existence Absolute. I am the Bliss Absolute, One without a second and the Innermost Consciousness.

Remaining in this state of absolute identification is what is called '*Samādhi*'[2] or the Super-conscious state.

1 *Should be resolved etc.*—See verses 48-53.
2 '*Samādhi*'—See verse 48, note 1, and verse 51, note 3.

'तत्त्वमसि' 'ब्रह्माहमस्मि' 'प्रज्ञानमानन्दं ब्रह्म' 'अयमात्मा ब्रह्म' इत्यादिश्रुतिभ्यः। इति पञ्चीकरणं भवति ॥

इति श्रीशङ्कराचार्यविरचितं पञ्चीकरणम् ।

तत् त्वम् असि 'Thou art That', ब्रह्म अहम् अस्मि 'I am Brahman', प्रज्ञानम् आनंदं ब्रह्म 'Consciousness-Bliss is Brahman', अयम् आत्मा बृह्म 'This Self is Brahman' इति-आदि-श्रुतिभ्य: these 'Śrutis', i.e., the Upaniṣadic sayings are direct evidences to the identity of the Ātman, the individual soul and Brahman. इति भवति This is what is called पञ्चीकरणम् '*Pañcīkarṇam*' or quintuplication. इति Here ends, पञ्चीकरणम् the small treatise named '*Pañcīkaraṇam*' श्रीशङ्कराचार्य-विरचितम् composed by Bhagavan Śrī Śaṅkarācārya.

'Thou art That', 'I am Brahman', 'Consciousness-Bliss is Brahman', 'This Self is Brahman', etc.—all these[1] *Śrutis.*, i.e., the *Upaniṣadic* sayings are direct evidences to the identity of the Ātman, the individual soul, and Brahman. This is what is called '*Pañcīkaraṇam*' or quintuplication.

Here ends the small treatise named '*Pañcīkaraṇam*', composed by Bhagavān Śrī Śaṅkarācārya'.

1 These are called '*Mahāvākyas*'. Properly understood and realized, anyone of these sets an aspirant immediately free from ignorance, which is the cause of all bondage. There are four principal

Mahāvākyas, directly communicating the knowledge of the identity of Jīva and Brahman, viz

(*i*) 'तत्त्वमसि'—Thou art That. Ch. 6, 8, 7.

(ii) 'अहं ब्रह्मास्मि'—I am Brahman. Bṛ. 1, 4, 10.

(*iii*) 'प्रज्ञानं ब्रह्म'—Consciousness is Brahman. Ai. 5, 3.

(*iv*) 'अयमात्मा ब्रह्म'—This Self is Brahman. Mā. 1, 2; Bṛ. 5, 19.

ॐ

श्रीसुरेश्वराचार्यकृत-पञ्चीकरणवार्त्तिकम्

Śrī Sureśvarācārya's Vārttika on Pañcīkaraṇam

Practice of *Samādhi* (i.e., the attainment of the knowledge of the unity of the individual and the Universal Soul) with the help of '*Aum*' has been enjoined by the scriptures[1] on those aspirants after liberation who have purified their minds by doing selfless work (in a spirit of worship to God), have abstained from forbidden deeds, have given up all earthly and heavenly desires, have got the power of discrimination between the Real and the unreal, and have gone through the six-fold[2] discipline of Śama, Dama, etc. Such seekers after truth, after renouncing everything give themselves up completely to constant hearing, reasoning and meditating on the Ātman. Bhagavān Śrī Śaṅkarācārya has shown very succinctly in his small treatise, '*Pañcīkaraṇam*', the way of attaining this knowledge through meditation on '*Aum*'. Sureśvarācārya, his worthy disciple, elaborates that by composing the following verses:

ओंकारः सर्ववेदानां सारस्तत्त्वप्रकाशकः ।
तेन चित्तसमाधानं मुमुक्षूणां प्रकाश्यते ॥१॥

ओंकारः The syllable '*Aum*' is, सारः the essence, सर्ववेदानां of all the Vedas, and तत्त्वप्रकाशकः reveals the highest Truth. चित्तसमाधानं The method of merging the mind in the idea of oneness with Brahman, तेन with the aid of that '*Aum*' प्रकाश्यते is being explained here, मुमुक्षूणां for the guidance of the aspirants after liberation.

1. '*Aum*'[3] is the essence of all the Vedas and reveals the highest Truth. The method of concentration of mind through that '*Aum*' is hereby being expounded for the sake of the aspirants after liberation.

1 *Scriptures*—Which speak that Jīva and Brahman are identical and the universe is unreal. These are called Śruti or Vedānta, the concluding and knowledge-portion of the Vedas. Śruti is the only right evidence with regard to the knowledge of the Self-Brahman. No wrong, futile or doubtful knowledge can arise out of the teachings of the Śrutis.

2 *Six-fold discipline*—Keeping under control (*i*) the internal organs (शम); (*ii*) external organs (दम); (*iii*) renouncing all worldy actions and embracing a monastic life (उपरति); (*iv*) endurance (तितिक्षा); (*v*) profound contemplation (समाधान); and (*vi*) unflinching faith in the words of the Teacher and Vedānta (श्रद्धा). As house-holders have got very little time to go through all these disciplines, as enumerated above, some are of opinion that monks alone are qualified to attain the Knowledge of Brahman through the method as prescribed in this book. (See Gītā, 18, 49—Śaṅkarānanda's commentary.)

3 *Aum*—The sound '*Aum*' is the name and symbol of Brahman (See Ka. 1. 2. 16-17). One realizes Brahman by meditating on this '*Aum*' after fully understanding all its implications as stated in this book. When '*Aum*' is uttered with concentration there arises the consciousness of Brahman in the mind. The different parts of the vocal organ used in uttering various sounds come in contact with one another while pronouncing the word '*Aum*'. Hence '*Aum*' is the matrix of all sounds. Brahman is the substratum of the whole universe and '*Aum*', too, is the substratum of all sounds as stated above. Sounds and phenomena are non-different, both being illusions. So the substratum alone remains. Hence Brahman is '*Aum*' (Mā. 1).

2. In Vedānta the method of 'illusory'[1] attribution, "*Adhyāropa*" and its negation, "*Apavāda*", is often used as a way to arrive at the Truth. Here the author first describes the unalloyed Consciousness, and then how it appears to be tainted by fictitious notions called '*Adhyāropa*'.

आसीदेकं परं ब्रह्म नित्यमुक्तमविक्रियम् ।
तत्स्वमायासमावेशाद्बीजमव्याकृतात्मकम् ।।२।।

परं ब्रह्म The Supreme Brahman, नित्य-मुक्तम् eternally free, अविक्रियम् and immutable, एकं आसीत् existed alone. तत् That Brahman, स्व-माया-समावेशात् owing to the superimposed identity with Its own, Māyā, the Cosmic Energy, which is also falsely attributed to it, बीजम् constitutes the seed of the universe, अव्याकृत-आत्मकम् which is undifferentiated.

The Supreme Brahman[2], eternally free and immutable existed[3] alone. That owing to the superimposed identity with Its own Māyā[4] became, as it were, the seed[5] of the universe as the unformed and the un-named.

1 *Illusory attribution—'Adhyāropa'*, etc. :

'अध्यारोपापवादाभ्यां निष्प्रपञ्चः प्रपञ्च्यते ।
मुमुक्षुबोधसिद्ध्यर्थं तत्त्वज्ञैः कल्पितः क्रमः ।।'

i.e.—"By the method of illusory attribution and its negation the formless Brahman is expounded. For the communication of knowledge to the seekers after liberation this particular order has been prescribed by the wise ones."

So, '*Adhyāropa*' means falsely attributing one thing to another. Like seeming water in a mirage we consider Brahman, which is not the material world, to be the material world.

3

'*Apavāda*' is the negation of this wrong imputation. See verse 41, note 1.

2 *Supreme Brahman*—Brahman or Self, the all-comprehensive Principle, the only Reality, is of the nature of (a) Existence ('सदेव सौम्येदमग्र आसीत्'—This universe, my child, was in the beginning as Existence. Ch. 6. 2. 1), (*b*) Knowledge ('सत्यं ज्ञानमनन्तं ब्रह्म'—Brahman is Existence, Knowledge and Infinity. Tai 2.1) and (*c*) Bliss ('विज्ञानमानन्दं ब्रह्म'—Brahman is Consciousness and Bliss. Bṛ. 3. 9. 28). Apart from Brahman everything else is unreal and is superimposed on It.

3 *Existed*—The past tense is used to denote our ordinary view that things here had a beginning and came out of Brahman. But Brahman has neither beginning nor end, and the world of Phenomena is without real beginning or end in itself.

4 *Māyā*—It is the Power of Brahman transforming itself into the universe and is the cause of all illusions. *Sattva*, *Rajas* and *Tamas* are the three constituent essences of Māyā. It is neither real nor unreal and hence inexplicable. It cannot be proved by reasoning which is itself a product of ignorance or Māyā. And with the knowledge of the identity of Jīva and Brahman Māyā disappears just as the mistaken idea of a snake (in a rope-snake) is removed by the right knowledge of the rope (See Viv. Cū. 108-110).

Cf. 'अविद्याया अविद्यात्व इदमेव तु लक्षणम् ।
यत्प्रमाणासहिष्णुत्वमन्यथा वस्तु सा भवेत् ॥'

बृह० वा० १८१

The characteristic of ignorance is its very unintelligibleness. It cannot bear any proof or it will be a real thing (Bṛ. Vār. 181).

'सेयं भ्रान्तिर्निरालम्बा सर्वन्यायविरोधिनी ।
सहते न विचारं सा तमो यद्वद्दिवाकरम् ॥'

नै० सि० ३।६६

This illusion is without support and contradictory to all reasoning. It cannot bear any reasoning just as darkness cannot stand the sun (Nai. Si. 3.66).

So, just like the fanciful imagination of a snake in a rope. ignorance, too, is considered indescribable by the wise (Panc. 6.246.)

5 *Seed etc.*—Brahman, the Pure, Unalloyed Consciousness is neither the cause nor the effect of anything. Only when it is associated with Its own power, Māyā, It (सगुण-ब्रह्म) is said to be Iśvara, the cause of the universe.

3. How the unconditioned Brahman appears to be the cause of the universe has been depicted in the preceding verse. Now the process of gradual superimposition of the so-called creation on It is being demonstrated :

तस्मादाकाशमुत्पन्नं शब्दतन्मात्ररूपकम् ।
स्पर्शात्मकस्ततो वायुस्तेजोरूपात्मकं ततः ॥३॥
आपो रसात्मिकास्तस्मात्ताभ्यो गन्धात्मिका मही ।

तस्मात् From that Supreme Brahman, उत्पन्नं originated, आकाशम् Ether, शब्द-तन्मात्र-रूपकम् which is of the nature of sound. ततः From Ether, वायुः Air, स्पर्शात्मकः having the characteristic of touch, came into existence. ततः Thence again, तेजः Light, रूपात्मकं characterised by form was produced. From Light arose, आपः Water, रसात्मिकाः of the nature of taste. ताभ्यः From water came out मही Earth, गन्धात्मिका characterised by smell.

From That originated Ether[1] which is characterised by sound. From Ether, Air, having the characteristic of touch, came into existence. Thence again Light, characterised by form was produced. From Light arose

Water, of the nature of taste. From Water came out Earth with its distinctive quality of smell.

1 *Ether*— 'तस्माद्वा एतस्मादात्मनः आकाशः सम्भूतः'—From the Self has evolved Ether (Tai. 2. 1. 1). Cf. Mu. 1.1.7, Tai. 3.1, Gītā, 10.8.

4-6. The grosser the element the more are the qualities in it. Quality exclusive to each element, and also those retained by the succeeding elements from the preceding ones are being described here in a concise way :

शब्दैकगुणमाकाशं शब्दस्पर्शगुणो मरुत् ॥४॥
शब्दस्पर्शरूपगुणैस्त्रिगुणं तेज उच्यते ।
शब्दस्पर्शरूपरसगुणैरापश्चतुर्गुणाः ॥५॥
शब्दस्पर्शरूपरसगन्धैः पञ्चगुणा मही ।
तेभ्यः समभवत्सूत्रं भूतं सर्वात्मकं महत् ॥६॥

आकाशं Ether, शब्द-एक-गुणं has the quality of sound only. मरुत् Air, शब्द-स्पर्श-गुणः possesses two qualities, sound and touch. तेजः Light or Fire, उच्यते is said, त्रि-गुणं to have triple qualities, viz. शब्द-स्पर्श-रूप-गुणैः sound, touch and form. आपः Water, चतुर्-गुणाः has got four qualities, शब्द-स्पर्श-रूप-रस-गुणैः sound, touch, form and taste. मही Earth, पञ्च-गुणा is endowed with five qualities, शब्द-स्पर्श-रूप-रस-गन्धैः sound, touch, form, taste and smell. तेभ्यः From these subtle elements, समभवत् came into being, महत् the great, सर्वात्मकं universal, all-pervading, भूतं entity, सूत्रं called '*Sūtra*'.

Ether has the quality of sound[1] only. Air possesses the double qualities of sound and touch. Light or

Fire is said to have the triple qualities, sound, touch and form. Water has got four qualities— sound, touch, form and taste, whereas, Earth is endowed with five qualities, viz sound, touch, form, taste and smell. Out of all these subtle elements came into being the great, universal, all-pervading principle, called '*Sūtra*'[2].

1 *Sound only*—The subtle, i.e. the rudimentary, uncompounded elements have got their own characteristic respective qualities of sound, touch, form, taste and smell only.

2 '*Sūtra*'—'*Sūtra*' the total vital force before manifestation, is the soul that pervades the universe like a thread passing through the beads of a garland. It is also called '*Prāṇa*' for having the power of activity. "*Hiraṇyagarbha*" is its another name. Comp. the Sruti passages: 'हिरण्यगर्भः समवर्तताग्रे' —First *Hiraṇyagarbha* came into existence (Ṛg. Veda 10.121.1). 'हिरण्यगर्भं जनयामास पूर्वम्'—He first created *Hiraṇyagarbha* (Śv. 3.4). 'कतम एको देव इति प्राणः' —Which is that one deity—*Prāṇa* (Bṛ. 3.9.9).

The consciousness identifying itself with the aggregate of all subtle bodies is known as '*Sūtra*' or '*Hiraṇyagarbha*', whereas the consciousness associating itself with the individual subtle body is called '*Taijasa*'. In fact the same principle viewed collectively and individually appears as the two.

7. Like the origin of the subtle bodies from the subtle elementary constituents, the creation of the gross elements and bodies through their quintuplication is now being described:

ततः स्थूलानि भूतानि पञ्च तेभ्यो विराडभूत् ।
पञ्चीकृतानि भूतानि स्थूलानीत्युच्यते बुधैः ॥७॥

ततः From those subtle elements (originated), पञ्च the five, स्थूलानि gross, भूतानि elements. तेभ्यः From the gross elements, अभूत् was produced, विराट् the *Virāṭ*. बुधैः The learned, उच्यते describe, भूतानि the elements, स्थूलानि as gross, पञ्चीकृतानि after they undergo the fivefold combination.

Those subtle elements produced the gross ones, from which, again, the *Virāṭ*[1]—the Macrocosm or the objective totality—came into existence. The learned call the elements as gross only after their undergoing the process of quintuplication.[2]

1 *Virāṭ* or '*Vaiśvānara*' is the Consciousness which identifies, itself with all the gross bodies in the universe. See Verse 11, note 1.

2 *Quintuplication*—This will be explained in the succeeding verses.

8-10. The process of quintuplication is now being explained in the following three verses :

पृथिव्यादीनि भूतानि प्रत्येकं विभजेद्द्विधा ।
एकैकं भागमादाय चतुर्धा विभजेत्पुनः ।।८।।
एकैकं भागमेकस्मिन् भूते संवेशयेत्क्रमात् ।
ततश्चाकाशभूतस्य भागाः पञ्च भवन्ति हि ।।९।।
वाय्वादिभागाश्चत्वारो, वाय्वादिष्वेवमादिशेत् ।
पञ्चीकरणमेतत्स्यादित्याहुस्तत्त्ववेदिनः ।।१०।।

प्रत्येकं Each of the, भूतानि elements, पृथिव्यादीनि Earth etc., विभजेत् must be divided, द्विधा into two equal parts. एक-एकं भागम् One of these two parts, आदाय should be taken, पुनः and further, विभजेत् divided, चतुर्धा into four equal parts. एक-एकं भागम् Each of these latter four parts, संवेशयेत् should be added, क्रमात् in order,

एकस्मिन् भूते in the formation of each gross element. ततः च Thus, आकाशभूतस्य of the element Ether, भवन्ति हि there will be, पञ्च five, भागाः parts. Half of it will be Ether and the other half will consist of the चत्वारः four, वायु-आदि-भागाः parts contributed together by all the other four elements. एवम् Thus, आदिशेत् it is to be enjoined, वायु-आदिषु in the case of other elements like Air, etc. एतत् This, स्यात् is, पञ्चीकरणम् the process of fivefold combination, इति आहुः as said, तत्त्ववेदिनः by the wise.

Each of the several elements, Earth etc., must be divided into two equal parts. One of these two parts should be further split into four equal parts. Now to one half of each element should be added one quarter of each of the other four halved elements towards the formation of one gross element. Thus in Ether there will be five constituent parts. Half of it will be Ether and the other half will consist of the four parts contributed together by all the other four elements. Thus it is to be known in the case of the other four elements, like Air, etc. This process is the fivefold[1] combination according to the wise.

1 *Fivefold etc.*—i.e. quintuplication. The fiirst originated five subtle uncompounded elements cannot produce the gross objects of the universe. They have to go through this fivefold combination in the above-mentioned proportion to do the same. So, according to this process, although every gross element has got some part of the other elements too, in it —still it retains its own name owing to the preponderance of its own part.

(Br. Su. 2.4.22.)

11. That the compounded elements go into the formation of the gross Universe is being stated here :

पञ्चीकृतानि भूतानि तत्कार्यं च विराड् भवेत् ।
स्थूलं शरीरमेतत्स्यादशरीरस्य चात्मनः ॥११॥

भूतानि The gross elements, पञ्चीकृतानि are all compounded, च and, तत् कार्यं their effect, भवेत् is, विराट् *Virāṭ*. एतत् This, स्यात् is, स्थूलं the gross, शरीरम् body, अशरीरस्य च of the disembodied, आत्मनः Ātman.

The gross elements are all compounded. These produce the *Virāṭ*[1], i.e., the sum total of all the gross bodies. This is the gross body of the disembodied Ātman.

1 *Virāṭ*—Here '*Virāṭ*' means the aggregate of all the gross bodies. In fact, the Consciousness. associated with those bodies is what the word '*Virāṭ*' or '*Vaiśvānara*' denotes. (See verse 7, note 1.)

'विविधं राजमानत्वात् विराट्'—Because of its appearing as diverse in form It is called '*Virāṭ*'.

'विश्वेषु समस्तेषु नरेषु अहमित्यभिमानित्वात् वैश्वानरः'—Identifying Itself with all the individual souls It is known as '*Vaiśvānara*'.

12. The whole creation which is a superimposition on the Ātman is being shown in its threefold aspect:

अधिदैवतमध्यात्ममधिभूतमिति त्रिधा ।
एकं ब्रह्म विभागेन भ्रमाद्भाति न तत्त्वतः ॥१२॥

एकं The same indivisible, ब्रह्म Brahman, भाति appears, त्रिधा in three forms, विभागेन by division, भ्रमात्

through illusion, (and) न not, तत्त्वत: in reality. They are अधिदैवतम् the sphere of the gods, अध्यात्मम् the sphere pertaining to the body, अधिभूतम् इति and the sphere of the elements.

The one indivisible Brahman appears threefold through illusion and not in reality. These three forms are—'the sphere of the gods', 'the sphere pertaining to the body', and 'the sphere of the elements'.

13. That the respective gods associated with the particular senses set them in action is being stated here :

इन्द्रियैरर्थविज्ञानं देवतानुग्रहान्वितैः ।
शब्दादिविषयं ज्ञानं तज्जागरितमुच्यते ॥१३॥

इन्द्रियै: The senses, देवतानुग्रहान्वितै: aided by the respective gods, अर्थ-विज्ञानं give rise to the knowledge of objects. तत् That, ज्ञानं knowledge, coming through the apprehension of the, शब्द-आदि-विषयं external objects like sound, etc., उच्यते is said, जागरितम् to be the waking state.

The senses[1] being stimulated by the respective gods[2] give rise to the knowledge of objects. That knowledge coming through the apprehension of the external objects like sound, etc. is called the waking state.

1 *The senses*—i.e., the organs of perception together with the organs of action. (See verse 29.)

2 *The respective gods*—The macrocosm (ब्रह्माण्डम्) is represented in miniature in the microcosm (पिण्डाण्डम्). So the senses of knowledge and action do their work aided by the respective universal principles in the macrocosm, called gods.

14. For the sake of clear understanding, the three-fold division, mentioned previously, is being further illustrated in the following fifteen verses :

श्रोत्रमध्यात्ममित्युक्तं श्रोतव्यं शब्दलक्षणम् ।
अधिभूतं तदित्युक्तं दिशस्तत्राधिदैवतम् ॥१४॥

श्रोत्रम् The sense of hearing, उक्तं is said, अध्यात्मम् इति to be pertaining to the body, whereas, तत् that, श्रोतव्यं which is heard, शब्दलक्षणम् namely sound, अधिभूतम् इति belongs to the sphere of the elements, and दिश: the quarters i.e., the deities associated with them, तत्र in this connection, उक्तं are said, अधिदैवतम् to be pertaining to the sphere of gods.

The sense of hearing belongs to the body, whereas, what is heard, namely, sound, belongs to the sphere of the elements.[1] And the quarters[2], in this connection, are said to be included in the sphere of gods.

1 *The elements*—'*Adhibhūta*' here means the objects of the respective sense. The sense-organs originate from the *Sattva* quality of the subtle elements.

2 *And the quarters*—'दिश: श्रोत्रं भूत्वा कर्णौ प्राविशन्'—The quarters i.e., the deities associated with them entered the ears in the form of the sense of hearing (Ai. 2.4).

त्वगध्यात्ममिति प्रोक्तं स्प्रष्टव्यं स्पर्शलक्षणम् ।
अधिभूतं तदित्युक्तं वायुस्तत्राधिदैवतम् ॥१५॥

त्वक् The sense of touch, प्रोक्तं it is said, अध्यात्मम् इति belongs to the body and तत् that स्प्रष्टव्यं which is touched, स्पर्शलक्षणम् characterised by the sense of touch, अधिभूतम् इति pertains to the sphere of the elements. वायुः The deity associated with air, उक्तं is said, तत्र in this connection, अधिदैवतम् to be the presiding deity.

15. The sense of touch, it is said, belongs to the body and what is touched, characterised by the sense of touch pertains to the sphere of elements. And the god of air[1] is here the presiding deity.

1 *God of air*—'ओषधि-वनस्पतयो लोमानि भूत्वा त्वचं प्राविशन्' —Herbs and trees entered the skin in the form of the hairs (Ai. 1.4). Although cited in the Śruti as deities, herbs and trees are not known as such. So air, which dominates them, has been designated as the presiding deity here.

चक्षुरध्यात्ममित्युक्तं द्रष्टव्यं रूपलक्षणम् ।
अधिभूतं तदित्युक्तमादित्योऽत्राधिदैवतम् ।।१६।।

चक्षुः The sense of vision, उक्तम् is said, अध्यात्मम् इति to be belonging to the body and, तत् that, द्रष्टव्यम् which is seen, रूपलक्षणम् characterised by form, अधिभूतम् इति pertains to the sphere of the elements. आदित्यः The Sun-god, अत्र here, उक्तम् it is said, अधिदैवतम् belongs to the sphere of gods.

16. The sense of vision belongs to the body. That which is seen, characterised by form, pertains to the sphere of elements and the Sun[1] is the corresponding deity in the sphere of the gods.

1 *The Sun*—'आदित्यश्चक्षुर्भूत्वाऽक्षिणी प्राविशत्'—The Sun-god, in the form of the sense of seeing, entered the eyes.—Ai. 2.4.

जिह्वाऽध्यात्मं तयाऽऽस्वाद्यमधिभूतं रसात्मकम् ।
वरुणो देवता तत्र जिह्वायामधिदैवतम् ॥१७॥

जिह्वा The sense-organ of taste, अध्यात्मम् belongs to the body, and आस्वाद्यम् what is tasted, रसात्मकम् having the property of taste, तया by the tongue, अधिभूतम् belongs to the sphere of elements. तत्र जिह्वायाम् In the tongue, देवता the god, वरुणः Varuṇa, अधिदैवतम् is the presiding deity.

17. The sense-organ of taste belongs to the body and what is tasted by the tongue belongs to the sphere of elements. Varuṇa[1], the god, is the presiding deity in the tongue.

1 *Varuṇa*—(रस)—Taste implies water which is dominated by the deity Varuṇa. —That Varuṇa, too, is a deity, is evident from the Śruti—'शं नो मित्रः शं वरुणः'—May Mitra, the deity who owns Prāna and Day: and Varuna, the deity who owns *Apāna* and Night, bestow on us all happiness.—Tai. 1.1.

घ्राणमध्यात्ममित्युक्तं घ्रातव्यं गन्धलक्षणम् ।
अधिभूतं तदित्युक्तं पृथिव्यत्राधिदैवतम् ॥१८॥

घ्राणम् The sense-organ of smell, उक्तम् is said, अध्यात्मम् इति as belonging to the body. तत् घ्रातव्यम् That which is smelt, गन्धलक्षणम् possessed of the nature of smell अधिभूतम् belongs to the sphere of elements. पृथिवी The Earth-god, उक्तम् is known, अत्र here, अधिदैवतम् as the presiding deity.

18. The sense-organ of smell is said to be belonging to the body. That which is smelt, possessed of

the nature of smell, belongs to the sphere of the elements, and the Earth-god[1] is here the presiding deity.

1 *Earth-god*—The sense-organ of smell is derived from the Earth. So the Earth-god has been said here to be the presiding deity. In the Śruti—'वायुः प्राणो भूत्वा नासिके प्राविशत्'—Air, in the form of *Prāṇa*, entered the nostril (Ai. 2.4.),—Air has been described as the deity of the organ of smell, still air-god should be understood as subsidiary to the Earth-god.

वागध्यात्ममिति प्रोक्तं वक्तव्यं शब्दलक्षणम् ।
अधिभूतं तदित्युक्तमग्निस्तत्राधिदैवतम् ॥१९॥

वाक् The organ of speech, प्रोक्तम् is said, अध्यात्मम् इति to be belonging to the body, whereas, तत् वक्तव्यम् that which is spoken, शब्दलक्षणम् of the nature of sound, अधिभूतम् belongs to the sphere of the elements. अग्निः The Fire-god, उक्तम् is said, अधिदैवतम् to be the presiding deity; तत्र there.

19. The organ of speech is said to be belonging to the body, whereas, that which is spoken, of the nature of sound, belongs to the sphere of elements. The Fire-god[1] is there the presiding deity.

1 *Fire-god*—'अग्निर्वाग् भूत्वा मुखं प्राविशत्'—The Fire-god, in the form of the organ of speech, entered the mouth.—Ai. 2.4.

Like the five organs of perception, the five organs of action too, which originate from the '*Rajas*' quality of the subtle elements, have got their respective deities.

हस्तावध्यात्ममित्युक्तमादातव्यं च यद्भवेत् ।
अधिभूतं तदित्युक्तमिन्द्रस्तत्राधिदैवतम् ॥२०॥

हस्तौ The organ of hands, उक्तम् is said, अध्यात्मम् इति belongs to the body. तत् That, यत् आदातव्यं च which is handled, अधिभूतं is in the sphere of elements, and इन्द्र the god Indra, अधिदैवतम् is the presiding deity, तत्र there.

20. The organ of hands, it is said, belongs to the body. That which is handled is in the sphere of elements and the god Indra[1] is there the presiding deity.

1 *Indra*—'इन्द्रो मे बले श्रितः'—Indra is the god of my strength; and again, 'बाहुओर्बलम्'—Strength is considered to be contained in the arms. So, Indra is here described as the deity of the hands.

पादावध्यात्ममित्युक्तं गन्तव्यं तत्र यद्भवेत् ।
अधिभूतं तदित्युक्तं विष्णुस्तत्राधिदैवतम् ।।२१।।

पादौ The organ of feet, उक्तं is said, अध्यात्मम् इति to be in the body. यत् That which, भवेत् is, तत्र in this connection, गन्तव्यं the object or place gone to, तत् अधिभूतं belongs to the realm of the elements. विष्णुः God Viṣṇu अधिदैवतम् is the presiding deity, तत्र thereof.

21. The organ of feet is said to be pertaining to the body, whereas that, which is, in this connection, the object or place gone to, belongs to the realm of the elements. God Viṣṇu[1] is the presiding deity thereof.

1 *God Viṣṇu*— Viṣṇu in His Vāmana or Dwarf *Avatāra* is believed to have covered the whole universe by one stride in order to subdue Bali, the Deomon-King. Bali was tricked out of the dominion he had obtained over the earth and heaven

and left in consideration of his merits the sovereignty of the infernal regions. Viṣṇu is considered to be the god of the organ of feet.

पायुरिन्द्रियमध्यात्मं विसर्गस्तत्र यो भवेत् ।
अधिभूतं तदित्युक्तं मृत्युस्तत्राधिदैवतम् ।।२२।।

पायुः इन्द्रियम् The organ of excretion, अध्यात्मं is in the sphere of the body. यः That, which, भवेत् is, विसर्गः the excrescence, तत्र there, तत् अधिभूतं is of the sphere of the elements. मृत्युः The god of death, अधिदैवतम is the presiding deity, तत्र thereof.

22. The excretory organ is in the sphere of the body. Excrescence is of the sphere of the elements. The god of death is the corresponding presiding deity.

उपस्थेन्द्रियमध्यात्मं स्त्र्याद्यानन्दस्य कारणम् ।
अधिभूतं तदित्युक्तमधिदैवं प्रजापतिः ।।२३।।

उपस्थ-इन्द्रियम् The generative organ, अध्यात्मं belongs to the body. तत् That, कारणम् objective source, आनन्दस्य of pleasure, स्त्री-आदि like women etc., उक्तम् is said, अधिभूतं to be in the realm of elements. प्रजापतिः The god Prajāpati, अधिदैवम् is the deity.

23. The generative organ belongs to the body. The objective source of pleasure is the corresponding factor in the sphere of the elements. God Prajāpati[1] is the corresponding deity.

1 *Prajāpati*—Although in the Śruti—'आपो रेतो भूत्वा शिश्नं प्राविशन् —Water, in the form of the seminal fluid entered

the generative organ' (Ai. 2. 4)—water has been observed as the deity, still it is to be understood that by the word 'water' there, Prajāpati, the god of reproduction has been hinted at.

मनोऽध्यात्ममिति प्रोक्तं मन्तव्यं तत्र यद्भवेत् ।
अधिभूतं तदित्युक्तं चन्द्रस्तत्राधिदैवतम् ॥२४॥

मन The mind, प्रोक्तं is said, अध्यात्मम् इति to be in the realm of the body. यत् Whatever, तत्र there, भवेत् is, मन्तव्यं thought of, तत् that, उक्तं is said, अधिभूतं belongs to the world of elements. चन्द्रः The moon-god, अधिदैवतम् is the presiding deity, तत्र in the corresponding realm.

24. The mind is said to be in the realm of the body. Whatever is thought of, belong to the world of elements. The moon-god is the presiding deity of the mind.

बुद्धिरध्यात्ममित्युक्तं बोद्धव्यं तत्र यद्भवेत् ।
अधिभूतं तदित्युक्तमधिदैवं बृहस्पतिः ॥२५॥

बुद्धिः Intellect, the determinating factor, उक्तं is said, अध्यात्मम् इति to be in the sphere of the body. यत् Whatever, तत्र there, भवेत् is, बोद्धव्यं determined, तत् that, उक्तम् is said, अधिभूतम् इति pertains to the sphere of elements. बृहस्पतिः The god Bṛhaspati अधिदैवं is the presiding deity.

25. The determinative intellect is in the sphere of the body, whereas whatever is subject to determinative intellection belongs to the sphere of the elements, and

in the sphere of gods Bṛhaspati[1] stands as the presiding deity.

1 *Bṛhaspati*—That Bṛhaspati and others are also presiding deities has to be ascertained from the *Āgamas* (Tantras). Cf. 'बृहस्पतिरिव बुद्धचा'—May I become like Bṛhaspati in intellect.

अहंकारस्तथाऽध्यात्ममहंकर्तव्यमेव च ।
अधिभूतं तदित्युक्तं रुद्रस्तत्राधिदैवतम् ।।२६।।

अहंकारः The sense of ego, तथा likewise, अध्यात्मम् is in the bodily plane. तत् All that, अहंकर्तव्यम् एव च subject to the sense of ego, उक्तं is said, अधिभूतं to be belonging to the realm of the elements and, रुद्रः the god Rudra, अधिदैवतम् is the presiding deity, तत्र thereof.

26. Likewise, the sense of ego is in the bodily plane and all that concerning which the sense of ego is exercised belongs to the world of elements. The god Rudra, is the presiding deity.

चित्तमध्यात्ममित्युक्तं चेतव्यं तत्र यद्भवेत् ।
अधिभूतं तदित्युक्तं क्षेत्रज्ञोऽत्राधिदैवतम् ।।२७।।

चित्तम् The contemplative or reasoning faculty, उक्तं is said, अध्यात्मम् इति to be in the sphere of the body. यत् That which, भवेत् is, तत्र there, चेतव्यं the object of contemplation, तत् अधिभूतम् इति is in the sphere of the elements. क्षेत्रज्ञः The knower of the body, i.e. the individual witnessing consciousness, उक्तं is called, अधिदैवतम् the corresponding deity, अत्र in the sphere of the gods.

27. The reasoning faculty is said to be in the bodily realm and that which is the object of reasoning belongs to the sphere of the elements. The '*Kṣetrajña*' or the witnessing Consciousness is the corresponding deity in the sphere of the gods.

तमोऽध्यात्ममिति प्रोक्तं विकारस्तत्र यो भवेत् ।
अधिभूतं तदित्युक्तमीश्वरोऽत्राधिदैवतम् ।।२८।।

तमः Darkness, i.e. delusion, gloom or ignorance, प्रोक्तं it is said, अध्यात्मम् इति belongs to the sphere of the body, whereas, यः विकारः the mutations, भवेत् happening, तत्र therein, उक्तम् are said, तत् अधिभूतं to be in the elemental sphere. ईश्वरः The Supreme God-head, अधिदैवतम् is the presiding deity, अत्र here.

28. Ignorance[1], it is said, belongs to the bodily sphere, whereas the mutations happening therein are in the sphere of the elements. The supreme 'God-head'[2] is the presiding deity.

1 *Ignorance*—The causal body.
2 *God-head*—Īśvara, the cause of the world who controls Māyā.

बाह्यान्तःकरणैरेवं देवतानुग्रहान्वितैः ।
स्वं स्वं च विषयज्ञानं तज्जागरितमुच्यते ।।२९।।

एवं Thus, बाह्य-अन्तः-करणैः by the senses, both internal and external, and by the organs of action, देवता-अनुग्रह-अन्वितैः all guided by their corresponding deities, स्वं स्वं च विषयज्ञानं knowledge of the respective external objects, happens. तत् That, is what, उच्यते is called, जागरितम् the waking state.

29. Thus, by 'waking state' is meant the knowledge of the respective objects resulting from the operation of senses, both external and internal, aided by their corresponding deities.

30. The first letter 'A' of the syllable '*Aum*' represents the gross body, the waking state and the Consciousness called '*Viśva*' associated with them. Now the word '*Viśva*', of the text is being explained here :

येयं जागरितावस्था शरीरं करणाश्रयम् ।
यस्तयोरभिमानीस्याद्विश्व इत्यभिधीयते ।।३०।।

यः That which, स्यात् is, अभिमानी identified with तयोः the two namely, या इयम् जागरित-अवस्था this waking state, and the, शरीरं gross body, करण-आश्रयम् which is the seat of the senses, i.e. the subtle body, अभिधीयते is described, as, विश्वः इति the *Viśva*.

That which identifies Itself with both the waking state and the body[1], which is the seat of the senses, is described as the *Viśva*.

1 *The body*—In the waking state Consciousness identifies Itself with the gross body and in doing so, It evidently identifies Itself with the subtle body, which is contained by the former one. This has been hinted at by saying that the gross body is the seat of the senses (i.e. the subtle body). The causal body, ignorance, the basis of the subtle body, too, comes into the

picture and is identified with himself by *Viśva*. So, as a matter of fact *Viśva* identifies Itself with all the three bodies.

—'सुक्ष्मशरीरमपरित्यज्य स्थूलशरीरप्रवेष्टत्वात् विश्वः'—

Consciousness, having entered, as it were, the gross body without giving up Its identification with the subtle body is called '*Viśva*'.

31. Vedānta always strives to establish the identity of the individual and the Universal Soul.

In the preceding verse *Viśva* has been said to be one with the gross body, and in verse 11 it has been stated that the compounded elements go to form the *Virāṭ*. That this is possible only in case the two are identical is being described now.

विश्वं वैराजरूपेण पश्येद्भेदनिवृत्तये ।

विश्वं This *Viśva*, पश्येत् must be looked upon, वैराजरूपेण as *Virāṭ*, भेदनिवृत्तये so that the sense of the reality of duality may be removed.

This *Viśva*, (the individual Consciousness identifying Itself with the waking state and the gross body), must be looked upon as identical with *Virāṭ* (the Macrocosmic Consciousness) so that duality may be sublated.

31-34. In the following seven verses (31-37) the subtle body of the Ātman is being expounded :

ज्ञानेन्द्रियाणि पञ्चैव पञ्च कर्मेन्द्रियाणि च ।।३१।।
श्रोत्रत्वङनयनघ्राणजिह्वा धीन्द्रियपञ्चकम् ।
वाक्पाणिपादपायूपस्थाः कर्मेन्द्रियपञ्चकम् ।।३२।।

मनोबुद्धिरहंकारश्चित्तं चेति चतुष्टयम् ।
संकल्पाख्यं मनोरूपं बुद्धिर्निश्चयरूपिणी ।।३३।।
अभिमानात्मकस्तद्वदहंकारः प्रकीर्तितः ।
अनुसंधानरूपं च चित्तमित्यभिधीयते ।।३४।।

ज्ञान-इन्द्रियाणि The sense-organs of perception are, एव definitely, पञ्च five in number, च and, पञ्च five, कर्म इन्द्रियाणि are the organs of action. धी-इन्द्रिय-पञ्चकम् The five organs of perception, are the organs of श्रोत्र hearing, त्वक् touch, नयन seeing, घ्राण smell and, जिह्वा taste. कर्म-इन्द्रिय-पञ्चकम् The five organs of action, are the organs of, वाक् speech, पाणि the hands, पाद the feet, and the organs of, पायु evacuation and, उपस्थाः generation. There are चतुष्टयम् four, internal organs, च too, namely, मनः the mind, बुद्धिः the intellect, अहंकारः Egoism and, चित्तम् इति memory or the faculty of contemplation. मनोरूपं The mind, is that function of the internal organ which considers, संकल्पाख्यं the pros and cons of a subject, and बुद्धिः the intellect is that faculty, निश्चयरूपिणी which determines. तद्वत् Likewise, अहंकारः the principle of the ego, प्रकीर्तितः is said, अभिमानात्मकः to be of the nature of Self-Consciousness. चित्तम् इति The apparatus of contemplation, अभिधीयते is said to be that which, अनुसंधानरूपं च carries on contemplation.

The sense-organs of perception are five, viz the organs of hearing, touch, seeing, smell, and taste. The organs of action, too, are five, namely that of speech the hands, the feet and the organs of excretion and generation.

There are four internal organs[1], namely, the mind, the intellect, the ego and the apparatus of contemplation. The mind is that which considers the pros and cons[2] of a subject, and the intellect is that faculty which determines[3]. Likewise, the principle of ego is said to be of the nature of the serse of ownership, and *Citta* or memory is that factor which remembers.

1 *Internal organs*—The inner organ (*antaḥkaraṇa*) is called *Manas, Buddhi, Citta,* and Ego owing to its different functions: the *Manas* (मनस्) when it cannot determine an object; the *Buddhi* (बुद्धि) when it is assured of the nature of the object; the *Citta* (चित्त) when it remembers, and the Ego (अहंकार) when it identifies itself with the body as its own Self. (See Viv. Cū. 93,94).

2 *Pros and cons*—When a person cannot determine whether an object is this or that, and whether to perform a particular action or not, '*Manas*' or the mind is then said to be functioning.

3 *Determines*—The real nature of an object.

प्राणोऽपानस्तथा व्यान उदानाख्यस्तथैव च ।
समानश्चेति पञ्चैताः कीर्तिताः प्राणवृत्तयः ॥३५॥
खं वाय्वग्न्यम्बुक्षितयो भूतसूक्ष्माणि पञ्च च ।
अविद्याकामकर्माणि लिङ्गं पुर्यष्टकं विदुः ॥३६॥
एतत्सूक्ष्मशरीरं स्यान्मायिकं प्रत्यगात्मनः ।

प्राणः The *Prāṇa,* अपानः *Apāna,* तथा and, व्यानः *Vyāna,* तथा एव च and likewise, that which is, उदानाख्यः called *Udāna,* समानः च इति and also *Samāna*—all, एताः these, पञ्च five, कीर्तिताः are described, as the five, प्राणवृत्तयः vital forces. भूत-सूक्ष्माणि The subtle elements, are

च also, पञ्च five, namely, खं-वायु-अग्नि-अम्बु-क्षितयः ether, air, fire, water and earth. अविद्या Nescience, काम desire, and कर्म action, all these, पुरी-अष्टकं eight cities, विदुः are known, to constitute, लिङ्गं the '*Liṅga*' body. एतत् This '*Liṅga*' body, स्यात् is called, the मायिकं illusory, सूक्ष्मशरीरं subtle body, प्रत्यक्-आत्मनः of the innermost Self.

35-36. The *Prāṇa*[1], *Apāna*, *Vyāna*, *Udāna* and *Samāna* —all these are called the five vital forces. The subtle elements are also five in number, viz ether, air, fire, water and earth. All these five groups together with Nescience[2], desire and action, also called as eight[3] 'cities', go to form the '*Liṅga*'[4] body. This is the illusory[5] subtle[6] body of the innermost Self or Ātman.

1 *Prāṇa*—The same *Prāṇa*, the vital force, is called the *Prāṇa* while inhaling and exhaling; the *Apāna* while excreting; *Vyāna* while it pervades the entire body; *Udāna* when it helps passing out from the body and *Samāna* when it assimilates food and drink. *Prāṇa* is said to be seated at the tip of the nose. being directly felt there, *Apāna* in the excretory organ, *Vyāna* in the entire body, *Udāna* in the throat (generally the subtle body passes out through this exit), and *Samāna* in the middle part of the body.

2 *Nescience*—i.e. ignorance of our real nature as the blissful Self. This ignorance leads to desire, which pushes one into action, the cause of countless sufferings. For detailed description of ignorance, see verse 2, note 4.

3 *The eight cities*—(i) the five organs of perception, (ii) the five organs of action, (iii) the five vital forces, (iv) the five subtle rudimentary elements, (v) the inner organ consisting of the mind, intellect etc., (vi) Nescience, (vii) desire, and (viii) action.

4 *Liṅga body*—i.e. the subtle body. The word 'subtle body'

may, in ordinary parlance, mean something like a spirit or ghost, so in Vedānta, '*Liṅga*' body is a better term. It is formed out of the eight aforesaid constituents.

5 *Illusory*—This indicates that this body is not real.

6 *Subtle body*—Made up of the eight cities. See Bṛ. 2. 3. 5. 6.

37-38. The workings of the subtle body are being elaborated further—

करणोपरमे जाग्रत्संस्कारोत्थं प्रबोधवत् ॥३७॥
ग्राह्यग्राहकरूपेण स्फुरणं स्वप्न उच्यते ।
अभिमानी तयोर्यस्तु तैजसः परिकीर्तितः ॥३८॥

करण-उपरमे When the sense-organs are inactive, स्फुरण the illumination, ग्राह्य-ग्राहक-रूपेण appearing as both the subject and object, प्रबोधवत् along with the knowledge, जाग्रत्-संस्कार-उत्थं arising from the impressions left over by the waking state, उच्यते is called, स्वप्नः the dream state. यः तु अभिमानी That which identifies itself with, तयोः both the dream state and subtle body, परिकीर्तितः is called, तैजसः *Taijasa* or the radiant one.

Dream is the state conditioned by the inactitviy of the senses, the potency of the impressions of waking state and the functioning of consciousness in the role of both the subject and object. The ego, which has the sense of ownership in relation to both (the dream state and the subtle body), is called '*Taijasa*'.[1]

1 *Taijasa*— 'तेजसि वासनायामहंममाभिमानितया तृप्तो भवतीति तैजसः'—i.e., One who feels contented on getting identified with desires. Or 'तेजोमयान्तःकरणवृत्तिविशिष्टत्वात् तैजसः'—It is called *Taijasa* because of its being identified with the modifications of the inner organ which is full of light, i.e., ideas.

हिरण्यगर्भरूपेण तैजसं चिन्तयेद् बुधः ।

बुधः The wise one, चिन्तयेत् should look upon, तैजसं this *Taijasa*, हिरण्यगर्भ-रूपेण as *Hiraṇyagarbha*, the subtle objective totality.

The wise one should look upon this '*Taijasa*' as identified with '*Hiraṇyagarbha*'[1], the subtle objective totality.

1 *Hiraṇyagarbha*—See *Sūtra* on verse 6, note 2.

39-40. Thus explaining the subtle body, the dream state and the consciousness associated with them—all these together representing the letter 'U'—the author now proceeds to show the causal body, the state through which it is endowed with experiences, and the consciousness combined with both, in order to explain the last letter 'M' of 'Aum':

चैतन्याभासखचितं शरीरद्वयकारणम् ।।३९।।
आत्माज्ञानं तदव्यक्तमव्याकृतमितीर्यते ।
न सन्नासन्न सदसद्भिन्नाभिन्नं न चात्मनः ।।४०।।

चैतन्य-आभास-खचितं Bound up with the reflection of Pure Consciousness, आत्म-अज्ञानं the Nescience of the Ātman, शरीर-द्वय-कारणम the cause of both the gross and subtle bodies, constitutes अव्यक्तम् the Unmanifested. तत् that, ईर्यते is described as, अव्यक्तम् इति Undifferentiated, too. न सत् This is neither existent, न असत् nor non-existent. न सत् असत् nor both existent and non-existent. It is न भिन्न-अभिन्नं neither different from nor identical with, the आत्मनः Ātman.

Bound up with the reflection of Pure Consciousness, the Nescience[1] of the Ātman, the cause of the gross and subtle bodies constitutes the Unmanifested, also called Undifferentiated (i.e., un-named and un-formed). This is neither existent nor non-existent nor both existent and non-existent. It is neither different from, nor identical with the Ātman.

1 *Nescience*—See verse 2, note 3. *Māyā*, *Avidyā*, *Ajnāna*, *Avyakta*, *Avyākrta*, Ignorance, Nescience, *Prakrti*—these terms are often synonymously used.

न सभागं न निर्भागं न चाप्युभयरूपकम् ।
ब्रह्मात्मैकत्वविज्ञानहेयं मिथ्यात्वकारणात् ॥४१॥

It, this Nescience, is न neither, सभागं made up of parts, न nor, is it निर्भागं non-composite, न nor, च अपि उभय-रूपकम् even both composite and non-composite. मिथ्यात्व-कारणात् By virtue of its being unreal, ब्रह्म-आत्म-एकत्व-विज्ञान-हेयं it is destructible by the knowledge of the identity of Brahman and Ātman.

41. It is neither made up of parts, nor, is it non-composite, nor even both composite and non-composite. By virtue of its being unreal[1] it is liable to elimination by the comprehension of the identity of Brahman and Ātman.

1. *Unreal*—Because it is wrongly imputed to the Ātman. All wrong imputations, i.e., *Adhyāropa*, vanish at the dawn of the knowledge of the real nature of the thing. When a rope is known to be distinct from the snake in a rope-snake, the snake then is said to be unreal. It is, then neither in the rope nor elsewhere. The rope does not actually change into a snake, but

only appears to be so, an illusion caused by ignorance. This is called the '*Vivarta-vāda*'-theory, the only pivot on which the structure of the Advaita Vedānta philosophy stands. As a snake is the '*vivarta*' of a rope, so is the universe the '*vivarta*' of Brahman. This illusion, consisting of only name and form, can be removed only by the knowledge of Brahman. The removal of the illusion is called '*Apavāda*'. (अवस्थान्तरभानं तु विवर्तो रज्जुसर्पवत्—Appearing as something else is called '*Vivarta*', as in the case of a rope-snake. See—Panc. 13.9). See verse 2, note 1.

42. After expounding the nature of the causal body, the state (deep-sleep) associated with it is now being explained:

ज्ञानानामुपसंहारो बुद्धेः कारणतास्थितिः ।
वटबीजे वटस्येव सुषुप्तिरभिधीयते ।।४२।।

वटस्य इव Like the banyan tree, वट-बीजे in its seed, when ज्ञानानाम् all thoughts both of the waking and dream states, उपसंहारः are withdrawn, and when बुद्धेः the determinative intellect, कारणता-स्थितिः lapses into its causal condition—that state, अभिधीयते is called, सुषुप्तिः '*Suṣupti*' or deep-sleep.

On the analogy of the banyan tree in the seed, when all thoughts vanish and when the determinative intellect merges into its causal condition, the state of deep-sleep dawns.

1 *All thoughts vanish...etc.*—

All thoughts vanish in the state of final liberation, and sometimes in the waking state, too, when the mind is free of all ideas, but that cannot be said to be the deep-sleep state. The mind etc., gets merged in the causal condition, i.e., ignorance, at the time of deep-sleep, from which again, everything springs up during the waking and dream states.

अभिमानी तयोर्यस्तु प्राज्ञ इत्यभिधीयते ।
जगत्कारणरूपेण प्राज्ञात्मानं विचिन्तयेत् ॥४३॥

यः तु That which, अभिमानी identifies itself with, तयोः these two—the deep-sleep state and the causal body, Nescience, अभिधीयते is described, as प्राज्ञः इति *Prājña*. विचिन्तयेत् one should look upon, प्राज्ञः-आत्मानम् this Self, *Prājña*, जगत्-कारण-रूपेण as identified with *Īśvara*, the cause of the universe.

43. The personality which appropriates these two (the deep-sleep state and the causal body) is described as '*Prājña*'[1]. One should look upon this '*Prājña*' as one or identical[2] with the Great Cause of the universe, '*Īśvara*'.

1 *Prājna.:* Consciousness in a state of deep-sleep is termed as such. In the waking state the Self is called '*Viśva*', in the dream state '*Taijasa*', and in the deep-sleep state '*Prājna*'. In deep-sleep though the '*Prājna*' remains unified with Brahman, owing to its being covered with ignorance, its knowledge is limited—'प्रज्ञारूपम् चैतन्यमस्यास्तीति प्राज्ञः'—*Turīya* is beyond these three states, where the Soul, divested of all ignorance, becomes fully aware of its perpetual identity with Brahman.

2 *Identical etc.:* The knowledge of identity of the individual soul with the Universal one is the only thing that Vedānta aims at.

44. That all these manifold divisions like *Viśva*, *Taijasa*, etc. (being of illusory nature) do not actually mar the non-duality of the Absolute Self is being described now :

विश्वतैजससौषुप्त-विराट्-सूत्राक्षरात्मभिः ।
विभिन्नमिव संमोहादेकं तत्त्वं चिदात्मकम् ।।४४।।

एकं The One, तत्त्वम् Truth, चित्-आत्मकम् of the nature of Pure Consciousness, appears संमोहात् through illusion, विभिन्नम् इव as many, viz. विश्व-तैजस-सौषुप्त-विराट्-सूत्र-अक्षर-आत्मभिः *Viśva*, *Taijasa*, *Prājña*, *Virāṭ*, *Sūtrātmā* or *Hiraṇyagarbha* and *Akṣara*.

The Ultimate Reality which is of the nature of Pure Consciousness, though one, appears, through illusion as the multitude[1] of *Viśva*[2], *Taijasa*, *Prājna*, *Virāṭ*, *Sūtra* and *Akṣara* forms.

1 *Multitude etc.*: Duality appears only owing to the illusory limiting adjuncts.
2 *Viśva etc.* : See verses 30 and 43, note 1.
3 *Virāṭ* : See verse 7, note 1, and verse 11, note 1.
4 *Sūtra* : See verse 6 note 2.
5 *Akṣara* : i.e. *Īśvara*, the Consciousness associated with the collective causal body. See verse 2, note 4, 5.

45. In reality Truth is only One and That, through illusion, appears as many. The way to attain this knowledge through the process of *Apavāda*[1], i.e., sublation, is being shown now:

विश्वादिकत्रयं यस्माद्वैराजादित्रयात्मकम् ।
एकत्वेनैव संपश्येदन्याभावप्रसिद्धये ।।४५।।

विश्व-आदिक-त्रयं The three individual forms—*Viśva*, *Taijasa* and *Prājña*, संपश्येत् must be contemplated, एकत्वेन एव as absolutely identical with, वैराज-आदि-त्रय -

आत्मकम् the corresponding collective three, namely, *Virāṭ*, *Sūtrātmā* and *Akṣara*, यस्मात् so that, अन्य-अभाव-प्रसिद्धये the non-existence of the difference of the entities may be established.

The three forms, *Viśva*, *Taijasa* and *Prājña*, must be contemplated as identical with *Virāṭ*, *Sūtrātmā* and *Akṣara*, respectively, so that the non-existence[2] of the difference of those entities may be established.

1 *Apavāda:* It is the negation of the illusory super-imposition, consisting of only name and form, and the consequent discovery of Brahman, the underlying Reality. See verse 2, note 1 and verse 41, note 1.

2 *Non-existence etc.:* The three individual forms of consciousness, after sublation, become identical with the three collective forms of Consciousness, and so only the latter three remain in place of six. How these three also are progressively reduced into One Pure Consciousness will be shown later.

46. Here the identity of words and their meanings are being shown so that by way of sublating the above three as described in the preceding verse, the words, too, will get merged in Pure Consciousness simultaneously:

ॐकारमात्रमखिलं विश्वप्राज्ञादिलक्षणम् ।
वाच्यवाचकताभेदाद्भेदेनानुपलब्धितः ॥४६॥

अखिलं The entire universe, विश्व-प्राज्ञ-आदि-लक्षणम् constituted by the three selves *Viśva*, *Taijasa* and *Prājña*, ॐकारमात्रम् is nothing but the syllable '*Aum*', वाच्य-वाचकता-अभेदात् there being no difference between the name and the named, भेदेन अनुपलब्धितः and also because they are not found in mutual separation.

'Aum' is the entire[1] universe constituted by the three selves, *Viśva*, *Taijasa* and *Prājña*. This is so because there is no ultimate difference between the name and the named[2] (entity) and also because the two are never cognized in mutual separation.

1 *Entire universe :*
A = *Viśva* + individual gross body + waking state
U = *Taijasa* + " subtle " + dream state
M = *Prajna* + causal " + deep-sleep state
Cf. Mā.1.1-12

2 *Name and named* See verse 1 note 3.
Cf. ('तद्यथा शंकुना . .' Ch.2.23.3) as leaves are covered by arteries, so all name e ervaded by 'Aum'.

Cf. ('वाचारम्भणं विकारो नामधेयम् . . . .' The modification being only a name arising from speech). Ch. 6.1.4.

47. The identity of 'Aum' in general with the whole universe has been spoken of. Now the parts (A, U, M) are being shown as one with their respective meanings:

अकारमात्रं विश्वः स्यादुकारस्तैजसः स्मृतः ।
प्राज्ञो मकार इत्येवं परिपश्येत्क्रमेण तु ॥४७॥

अकार-मात्रं The letter 'A' in 'Aum', स्यात् is, विश्वः *Viśva*, and उकारः the letter 'U', स्मृतः is considered, as तैजसः *Taijasa*, while the last मकारः letter 'M', प्राज्ञ इति is one with *Prājña*. एवं Thus these constituents of 'Aum' and the three selves, परिपश्येत् तु must be comprehended, क्रमेण in the proper order.

The constituent letter 'A' is '*Viśva*' and the letter 'U' is to be considered as '*Taijasa*', while the last letter 'M' is one with '*Prājña*'. Thus the identity of these constituent parts of 'Aum' and the three selves must be comprehended in the proper order.

48. So far contemplation prepara ory to *Samādhi* (a state of absorption with the Ultimate Truth) has been described. Now the process which immediately leads to that state is being narrated :

समाधिकालात्प्रागेवं विचिन्त्यातिप्रयत्नतः ।
स्थूलसूक्ष्मक्रमात्सर्वं चिदात्मनि विलापयेत् ।।४८।।

एवं Thus, प्राक् even prior to, समाधिकालात् the time of *Samādhi* or realization due to the merging of the mind in Pure Consciousness, विचिन्त्य contemplating on this Truth, अति-प्रयत्नतः with great care, विलापयेत् one should resolve, सर्वं all these, स्थूल-सूक्ष्म-क्रमात् in the order of gross, subtle and causal states, चिदात्मनि into the Supreme Ātman which is of the nature of Pure Consciousness.

Even prior to the time of *Samādhi*[1] contemplating on this Truth with great[2] care, one should resolve all these progressively in the order of gross, subtle and causal states into the Supreme Ātman which is of the nature of Pure Knowledge.

1 *Samādhi :* The state of complete absorption in the Abso ute and non-dual Brahman, arrived at as a result of discrimination and deep contempla ion with the help of 'Aum' as stated here.

2 *With great care* Because such contemplation can be done by one with unswerving perseverance, patience, faith and renunciation only.

49. How these are to be progressively merged into the Pure Consciousness, is being shown here:

अकारं पुरुषं विश्वमुकारे प्रविलापयेत् ।
उकारं तैजसं सूक्ष्मं मकारे प्रविलापयेत् ॥४६॥
मकारं कारणं प्राज्ञं चिदात्मनि विलापयेत् ।

पुरुषं The personality of, विश्वम् *Viśva,* अकारं which is one with 'A' in 'Aum', प्रविलापयेत् must be resolved into, उकारे 'U', i.e. into the dream Consciousness, *Taijasa.* सूक्ष्मं The subtle, तैजसं dream Consciousness, the *Taijasa,* उकारं the 'U' in 'Aum', प्रविलापयेत् must be merged into, मकारे the 'M' i.e. into the deep-sleep Consciousness, and again प्राज्ञ the *Prājña,* that deep-sleep Consciousness, कारणं who is the causal personality, and मकार known as 'M', विलापयेत् must be finally reduced to, चिदात्मनि the Ātman, of the nature of Pure Consciousness.

The waking-personality of '*Viśva*', symbolised by 'A' must be resolved into 'U' (i.e., the dream-personality). The subtle radiant personality of dream, the '*Taijasa*' symbolised by 'U' must be merged into 'M' (i.e., the personality of deep-sleep). Again the '*Prājña*', that deep-sleep Consciousness symbolised by 'M' and which is the causal personality must be finally reduced[1] to the Ātman, of the nature of Pure Consciousness.

1 *Finally reduced etc.*—This sort of meditation is called 'लय उपासना', or 'अहंग्रह उपासना'—meditation with the help of the sacred 'Aum'.

50-51. It has been said how the whole universe has to be reduced to the Supreme Ātman which is of the nature of Pure Consciousness. Now by way of showing the process of attaining the '*Samprajñāta Samādhi*', the essential characteristics of the Ātman are being presented here :

चिदात्माऽहं नित्यशुद्धबुद्धमुक्तसदद्वयः ॥५०॥
परमानन्दसंदोहवासुदेवोऽहमोमिति ।
ज्ञात्वा विवेचकं चित्तं तत्साक्षिणि विलापयेत् । ॥५१॥

अहं I am, चित् आत्मा the Ātman, the Pure Consciousness, नित्य-शुद्ध eternally pure, बुद्ध eternally enlightened, मुक्त ever free, and सत् One Existence, अद्वयः without a second. परमानन्दसंदोहः I am the Bliss Infinite. अहम् I am, वासुदेवः Vāsudeva—the all-pervading Supreme Spirit, and ॐ (I am) 'Aum'. इति ज्ञात्वा Thus comprehending, विवेचकं चित्तं the discerning contemplating faculty, विलापयेत् must also be resolved, तत् साक्षिणि into that final witness, the ultimate Ātman.

I am the Ātman, the Pure Consciousness, eternally pure and Intelligence Absolute, ever free and One without a second. I am the Bliss Infinite[1]. I am Vāsudeva[2], the all-pervading Supreme Spirit and I am 'Aum'. Thus[3] comprehending, the contemplative faculty[4] must also be merged into that final Witness[5], the Absolute Ātman.

1 ***Bliss Infinite*** **:** All enjoyments culminate in Brahman which is of the nature of Supreme Bliss. Cf. Bṛ. 4.3.32. The *Avyakta* or the *Akṣarātmā* is as it were, a part of Brahman

through the limiting adjunct ignorance; the *Sūtrātmā* or the Cosmic mind is again a part of that *Avyakta*, and the *Virāṭ*, i.e., the Cosmic soul identified with the gross universe is considered to be a fraction of the *Sūtrātmā*. Even the bliss of the *Virāṭ*-hood is something beyond the comprehension of the finite minds of ours. So Brahman is Bliss Infinite.

2 *Vāsudeva* : 'सर्वत्रासौ समत्वेन वसत्यत्रेति वै यतः । अतः स वासुदेवेति विद्वद्भिः परिपठ्यते ।।' As He (the Supreme Spirit) evenly pervades everything, so the wise ones call Him Vāsudeva. (*Viṣṇu Purāṇa*).

3 *Thus comprehending:* Here the process of attaining 'असंप्रज्ञात-समाधि' or *Nirvikalpa Samādhi* is being described. Thus comprehending—i.e. after practising the *Savikalpa Samādhi* for long. *Savikalpa Samādhi* is that state where the mind assumes the form of Brahman and rests on it with the distinction between the subject and object still persisting. When with the deepening of that state the duality of subject and object vanishes altogether, and the aspirant becomes one with Brahman, the state of *Nirvikalpa Samādhi* is said to have been achieved. So the former kind of *Samādhi* culminates into this.

4 *Contemplative faculty* : i.e., the faculty involving the three-fold divisions of meditation, meditator and the meditated.

5. *Witness* : 'स्वाध्यस्तान् पदार्थान् साक्षात् वृत्तिव्यवधानं विना आपरोक्ष्येण ईक्षते प्रकाशयतीति साक्षी'—'Because it directly illumines everything superimposed on it without the mediacy of any modification of the mind—it is called the Witness.

52 The state of '*Nirvikalpa Samādhi*' is being narrated now:

चिदात्मनि विलीनं चेत्तच्चित्तं नैव चालयेत् ।
पूर्णबोधात्मनाऽऽसीत पूर्णाचलसमुद्रवत् ।।५२।।

चेत् If, चित्तं the contemplating mind, विलीनम् is

merged, चित् आत्मनि into the Ātman, the Pure Consciousness then, तत् that, न एव चालयेत् should not be disturbed. आसीत One should remain, पूर्ण-बोध-आत्मना as that Infinite Consciousness, पूर्ण-अचल-समुद्रवत् like the full and motionless ocean.

When the contemplative mind is merged into the Ātman, the Pure Consciousness, then it should not be disturbed. One should then remain[1] as that Infinite Consciousness like the full and motionless ocean.

1 *One should then remain*—Cf. 'शमप्राप्तं न चालयेत्' etc. When the mind, free from all obstacles, is controlled, do not distract it any more. Do not linger on the bliss that comes from the *Savikalpa Samādhi* but be unattached through discrimination (Mā. Kārikā. 3.44).

53. Constant practice of this *Samādhi* gradually culminates in realization:

एवं समाहितो योगी श्रद्धाभक्तिसमन्वितः ।
जितेन्द्रियो जितक्रोधः पश्येदात्मानमद्वयम् ॥५३॥

एवं Thus practising, योगी a Yogi, i.e., an aspirant after Self-knowledge, समाहितः having attained perfect absorption, श्रद्धा-भक्ति-समन्वितः endowed with faith and devotion, जित-इन्द्रियः, जित-क्रोधः having overcome the senses and anger, पश्येत् perceives, आत्मानम् the Ātman, अद्वयम् One without a second.

Thus attaining perfect absorption through constant practice, an aspirant, endowed with faith[1] and devotion, and having overcome the senses and anger, perceives (realizes)[2] the Ātman, the One without a second.

1 *Endowed with faith and devotion :* These virtues have to be constantly and most reverentially practised for long till realization dawns: 'स तु दीर्घकाल-नैरन्तर्य-सत्कारासेवितो दृढभूमिः' —Firmness of the ground is achieved through long and constant practice with love. Yo. Sū. 1.14.

Comp.—'शान्तो दान्तः' etc., Quiet, subdued etc. (Bṛ. 4.4.23), also Mu. 1. 2. 11, Subāt. 9.1.4, Up. Sāh. 1. 3 .24; 16. 72.

2. *Perceives (realizes)* : Perfect maturity of the absorption is succeeded by realization.

54 It may be argued that such constant practice is not possible in the presence of mundane duties. In reply it is being brought to our notice that renunciation of, or aversion to, all perishable objects, the most important pre-requisite for an aspirant, has to be developed firmly right through the period of that practice :

आदिमध्यावसानेषु दुःखं सर्वमिदं यतः ।
तस्मात्सर्वं परित्यज्य तत्त्वनिष्ठो भवेत्सदा ॥५४॥

यतः As, इदं this empirical world, सर्वम् in its entirety, दुःखं is of the nature of sorrow, आदि-मध्य-अवसानेषु in the beginning, in the middle and in the end, तस्मात् so, परित्यज्य renouncing, सर्वम् everything, भवेत् one should be, सदा always, तत्त्व-निष्ठः established in Truth.

This empirical world, as a whole, is of the nature of sorrow[1] in the beginning[2], in the middle, and in the end. Therefore, after renouncing[3] everything an aspirant should steadfastly be established in Truth.

1 *Nature of sorrow* : 'जन्ममृत्युजराव्याधिदु:खदोषानुदर्शनम्'—Reflection on the evils of birth, death, old age, sickness and pain. (Gitā. 13.8)—all these produce sorrows. Indifference to sense-objects is born of this reflection, and gradually one turns towards the Ātman for attaining freedom from all sorrows.

2 *In the beginning etc.* : 'अर्थानामर्जने क्लेश: क्लेशस्तत्परिरक्षणे। नाशे दु:खं व्यये दु:खं धिगर्थान् क्लेशकारिण: ।।'—Wealth is hard to acquire, its protection entails lots of worries, when lost or spent it becomes the cause of untold sorrows—Fie on such wealth ! (Panc. 7.139).

In this way everything has to be discriminated. Cf. Panc. 7.140,141.

3 *After renouncing* : 'एतम् वै तमात्मानं विदित्वा ब्राह्मणा: पुत्रैषणायाश्च वित्तैषणायाश्च लोकैषणायाश्च व्युत्थायाथ भिक्षाचर्यं चरन्ति ।।'—After knowing this very Ātman the Brāhmaṇas (i.e., aspirants after liberation), renounce all desires for progeny, wealth and the worlds, and lead the life of a wandering monk (Bṛ. 3.5.1). 'न कर्मणा न प्रजया न धनेन त्यागेनैके अमृतत्वमानशु: ।।'—Not by rituals, not by progeny or wealth, but by renunciation alone immortality has to be achieved. 'परीक्ष्य लोकान् कर्मचितान् ब्राह्मणो निर्वेदमायान्नास्त्यकृत: कृतेन। तद्विज्ञानार्थं स गुरुमेवाभिगच्छेत् समित्पाणि: श्रोत्रियं ब्रह्मनिष्ठम् ।।'—Arriving at the conclusion through reasoning that the worlds, acquired by rituals, are impermanent, a Brāhmaṇa (i.e. an aspirant) in a spirit of dispassion, renounces everything, knowing those rituals full well as not conducive to the attainment of Brahman. For the Knowledge of Brahman the aspirant must go with fuel in his hand (or some flowers, etc. as offerings, in a spirit of service and humility) to the Teacher who is endowed with Vedic learning and thoroughly merged in Brahman (Mu. 1. 2. 12). This knowledge does not come without being taught by a teacher.

55. Perfect satiety is the due outcome of realization:

यः पश्येत्सर्वगं शान्तमानन्दात्मानमद्वयम् ।
न तेन किंचिदाप्तव्यं ज्ञातव्यं वावशिष्यते ॥५५॥

One, यः who, पश्येत् sees, सर्वगं the all-pervading, आनन्द-आत्मानम् Blissful Ātman, which is शान्तम् of the nature of peace, and अद्वयम् one without a second, तेन by him, न किंचित् nothing more, अवशिष्यते remains, आप्तव्यं to be attained, वा or, ज्ञातव्यं to be known.

For him, who sees the all-pervading Ātman, of the nature of supreme peace and bliss and the sole reality, there remains nothing more to be attained[1] and nothing more to be known[2].

1 *Nothing more to be attained :* all enjoyments or joys being included in the Bliss of Brahman, nothing more achievable is left behind. So a man of knowledge is free from all duties, and he is no longer bound by any injunction.

2 *Nothing more to be known :* because by knowing Him everything becomes known. Brahman alone, and nothing else, really exists. So when Brahman is known, nothing more remains to be known.

56. The state of perfection (where nothing more remains to be achieved or known) is further elucidated:

कृतकृत्यो भवेद्विद्वाञ्जीवन्मुक्तो भवेत्सदा ।
आत्मन्येवारूढभावो जगदेतन्न वीक्षते ॥५६॥

विद्वान् A wise one, भवेत् thus becomes, कृतकृत्यः perfect, and सदा eternally, जीवन्-मुक्तः free, although living.

आत्मनि एव आरूढभाव: Being thoroughly grounded in Ātman, he न does not, वीक्षते perceive, एतत् this, जगत् world.

A wise one attains the acme of life having nothing more to be achieved, and thus becomes eternally[1] free although still[2] living. With the whole of his mind and heart thoroughly filled with the Ātman, he does[3] not perceive this world.

1 *Eternally free:* During the time of *Samādhi* as well as when he is busy with outward activities.

2 *Still living :* This is called *Jīvanmukti*. When the knowledge of the Self-Brahman is attained, one is said to be liberated. But the body has to work out its pre-destined term of existence due to *Prārabdha*. So till the *Prārabdha* is exhausted through experience, such a man is called liberated while still living (*Jīvanmukta*). After the fall of the body the same is said to be *Videhamukta* (i.e., one who has attained disembodied or absolute freedom). Cf. Ka. 5. 1., Ch. 6. 14. 2. For "*Prārabdha*' Karma etc., see verse 58, note 4.

3 *Does not perceive:* Although he may perceive the appearance of the world comprising name and form, still, that has no reality for him and he is always fully conscious of Supreme Ātman, his real nature, the substratum of all illusory imputations.

57. That an emancipated soul is always free even while engaged in worldly activities is now being explained :

कदाचिद्व्यवहारे तु द्वैतं यद्यपि पश्यति ।
बोधात्मव्यतिरेकेण न पश्यति चिदन्वयात् ।।५७।।

कदाचित् Sometimes, यदि-अपि-तु even if, he पश्यति perceives, द्वैतं duality, व्यवहारे while engaged in outer activities, he न does not, पश्यति perceive it, बोध-आत्म-व्यतिरेकेण as different from the Ātman, of the nature of Consciousness, चित्-अन्वयात् for Consciousness pervades all.

Sometimes[1] even when he perceives duality in the ordinary course of life, he does[2] not really perceive it as different from the Ever-Conscious Ātman, for Consciousness runs in and through all.

1 *Sometimes:* i.e. when not in the state of *Samādhi.* An ignorant man always sees duality as real and is attached to it. To a man of knowledge the world comprising name and form appears no doubt, but that has no reality for him and he is also not lured by it.

2 *Does not really perceive it:* because whatever he perceives is just a false appearance. This false appearance of name and form is due to *Prārabdha* which has got to be exhausted through experience.

A man of knowledge does only what is good and beneficial for mankind. Although not bound by any law, the good habits, which he practised for long till the attainment of knowledge, persist, and he never transgresses the time-honoured customs and the sanctions of the scriptures. Śrī Sureśvarācārya says in his immortal book 'नैष्कर्म्य-सिद्धिः':

'बुद्धाद्वैतसतत्त्वस्य यथेष्टाचरणं यदि ।
शुनां तत्त्वदृशां चैव को भेदोऽशुचिभक्षणे' ।।४।६२।।

If a man, who has realized the non-dual Truth, goes out of bounds, then as regards consuming impure and forbidden things, what makes the difference between him and a dog? (4.62).

And again :

'उत्पन्नात्मावबोधस्य ह्यद्वेष्टृत्वादयो गुणाः ।
अयत्नतो भवन्त्यस्य न तु साधनरूपिणः' ।।४।६९।।

All qualities like non-violence etc., (Gītā, 12,13—19) attend a man of realization automatically and they have not to be practiced with effort. (4. 69.)

58. It has been said that the wise one never accepts duality as anything real. Now his angle of vision is further being illustrated :

किन्तु पश्यति मिथ्यैव दिङ्मोहेन्दुविभागवत् ।
प्रतिभासः शरीरस्य तदाऽऽप्रारब्धसंक्षयात् ॥५८॥

किन्तु Moreover, he पश्यति perceives the world of duality, मिथ्या-एव as unreal, दिङ्-मोह-इन्दु-विभाग-वत् even as one may see two moons, and mistake directions knowing full well the singleness of the moon and the correct identities of direction. प्रतिभासः The appearance, शरीरस्य of the body, तदा in that case, lasts आ-प्रारब्ध-संक्षयात् up to the completion of *Prārabdha.*

Moreover, a man of perfection perceives the world of duality as unreal even as one may see two moons[1] and mistake[2] directions though fully knowing the correct stand all the time. The illusion of his body lingers[3] up to the liquidation of his *Prārabdha*[4].

1 *Two moons :* Likewise the One Brahman appears as many due to various limiting adjuncts arising out of ignorance.

2 *Mistake directions :* The Supreme Ātman, similarly, is mistaken as the universe.

3 *Lingers up :* because false appearance cannot in any way contradict knowledge and liberation.

4 *Prārabdha :* There are three kinds of actions—viz
(*i*) *Sancita*—i.e., those accumulated in previous countless births.

(ii) *Āgāmi*—i.e. those that have yet to come, i.e., those that are done in this life after the attainment of knowledge.

(iii) *Prārabdha*—Part of the accumulated results of the past actions (i.e., *Sancita*) which has started bearing fruit by giving birth to the present body is called '*Prārabdha*'. The Knowledge of Brahman destroys all the results of the past accumulated actions (*Sancita*) and makes impotent those that are done after attainment of Knowledge (*Agāmi*), for, the realized man is not at all touched by them. But the *Prārabdha* persists and runs its own course by producing various experience till death. This is the state of *Jīvanmukti*. When the *Prārabdha* exhausts itself, the body of the liberated man falls and he attains the state of *Videha-mukti*, *i.e.* disembodied or Absolute liberation. See Br. Sū. 4. 1. 13-19.

59. What has been said in the previous verse is now being corroborated with the authority of the scriptures :

तस्य तावदेव चिरमित्यादि श्रुतिरब्रवीत् ।
प्रारब्धस्यानुवृत्तिस्तु मुक्तस्याभासमात्रतः ॥५९॥

श्रुतिः The Upaniṣad, अब्रवीत् says, that तस्य तावत् एव चिरम् इत्यादि "He, i.e., a man of Knowledge, has to wait only till he is delivered from the body, then he becomes united with Brahman". Ch. 6. 14. 2 etc. अनुवृत्तिः तु The persistence, प्रारब्धस्य of the *Prārabdha*, मुक्तस्य in the case of the liberated one, आभास-मात्रतः is only an appearance.

The Upaniṣad says, "As long[1] as the *Prārabdha* lasts" etc. The persistence of the *Prārabdha* in the case of the liberated one sustains only the appearance of the body etc., with no deluding potency.

1 *As long as* etc. : See verse 56, note 2, and verse 58, note 4. Ignorance is said to have two powers viz., the veiling power (आवरण-शक्ति) and the power of projection (विक्षेप-शक्ति), The former conceals the real nature of Brahman and the latter gives rise to the illusion of name and form. The knowledge of Brahman negates and completely destroys the veiling power, but the power of projection, although negated, i.e., known as false, persists till the exhaustion of the *Prārabdha* and gives rise to the appearances of name and form for that duration. A man of knowledge has to deal with these names and forms till death but he has no sense of reality in them. Even after the rope is known, it may resemble a snake but the sense of reality in the snake is gone for ever. Similarly, the appearance of the body and the world may persist but the balanced mind of a liberated man is not adversely affected by it. Cf.—Pleasure and pain do not touch one who is bodiless i.e., liberated. (Ch. 8. 12.1).

60. A man of Knowledge never accepts the appearance of duality presented by his *Prārabdha* as real, because :

सर्वदा मुक्त एव स्याज्ज्ञाततत्त्वः पुमानसौ ।

असौ That, ज्ञाततत्त्वः One who has known the truth, पुमान् man, स्यात् is, सर्वदा always, मुक्त एव free from all bondage.

One who has known the truth is always[1] free.

1 *Always:* i.e., not merely after the fall of the body but even when living; not merely when in *Samādhi* but even when engaged in outward activities. The moment one attains knowledge one verily becomes Brahman : 'ब्रह्म वेद ब्रह्मैव भवति'—(Mu.

3.2.9.) and so, inspite of the persisting appearance of the body etc., due to *Prārabdha,* such a person is not at all affected by them.

60-62. After his '*Prārabdha*' is exhausted through experience the enlightened one attains disembodied liberation :

प्रारब्धभोगशेषस्य संक्षये तदनन्तरम् ॥६०॥
अविद्यातिमिरातीतं सर्वाभासविवर्जितम् ।
आनन्दममलं शुद्धं मनोवाचामगोचरम् ॥६१॥
वाच्यवाचकनिर्मुक्तं हेयोपादेयवर्जितम् ।
प्रज्ञानघनमानन्दं वैष्णवं पदमश्नुते ॥६२॥

तत्-अनन्तरम् After, प्रारब्ध-भोग-शेषस्य the remaining *Prārabdha,* संक्षये is liquidated through experience, the liberated one, अश्नुते attains, पदम् the status, वैष्णवं of Viṣṇu, which is अविद्या-तिमिर-अतीतं free from the darkness of Nescience, सर्व-आभास-विवर्जितम् divested of all appearances, of the nature of अमलं stainless, आनन्दम् bliss, शुद्धं pure, मनो-वाचाम् अगोचरम् beyond mind and speech, वाच्य-वाचक-निर्मुक्तं above the distinctions of name and the named, हेय-उपादेय-विवर्जितम् neither to be shunned nor accepted, and प्रज्ञानघनम् is of the nature of Self-luminous Consciousness, and आनन्दम् Bliss.

After the residual *Prārabdha* has been gone through[1], the enlightened one attains that status of Visnu,[2] the Supreme Reality, attains that, wh'ch is free from the darkness of Nescience and divested[3] of all appearances, which is of the nature of stainless[4] consciousness and absolute purity, which transcends mind and speech and the distinctions of name and the named, which is neither to be shunned[5] nor to be accepted, and which is of the nature of self-luminous consciousness and Bliss.

1. *Gone through* : i.e., after the dissolution of his body.

2 *Viṣṇu* : The all-pervading Brahman, one without a second. See N. P. 5. 10, Cf. Va. Vr. 52. 53.

3 *Divested etc.* : This is the state of disembodied liberation where name and form do no longer appear at all.

4 *Stainless* : i.e., having no connection with ignorance or its effects.

5 *To be shunned* etc. : There being nothing apart from Ātman with whom the liberated soul is completely identified.

63. For the benefit of the seekers after liberation the pre-requisites, i.e., the absolutely necessary conditions for going through this course of *Sādhanā* (training) are being enumerated now :

इदं प्रकरणं यत्नाज्ज्ञातव्यं भगवत्तमैः ।
अमानित्वादिनियमैर्गुरुभक्तिप्रसादतः ॥६३॥

इदं This, प्रकरणं treatise, ज्ञातव्यं must be studied and properly understood, भगवत्तमैः under men of God-realization, यत्नात् with due care, अमानित्व-आदि-नियमैः after acquiring the qualities like humility etc., and गुरुभक्ति-प्रसादतः by evoking the grace of the teachers through devotional service.

This treatise[1] must be studied and properly understood under[2] men of God-realization. One must bring to bear on the study proper dispositions like humility,[3] loving service, etc., to the teacher.

1 *Treatise* : i.e., this '*Vārttika-Prakaraṇa*'. '*Vārttika*' is generally a collection of explanatory verses where things, spoken of in the main composition, are elucidated; things not spoken of, are illustrated, and things imperfectly stated, are clearly shown.

'*Prakaraṇa*' is a small work which deals concisely with the main theme, avoiding detailed consideration of the subject.

2 *Under men of God-realization* : An aspirant must go to a spiritual guide, a realized soul, for enlightenment. See verse 54, note 3.

Bhagavān Śrī Śaṅkarācārya in his commentary on the Mu. 1.2.12, says—'शास्त्रज्ञोऽपि स्वातन्त्र्येण ब्रह्मज्ञानान्वेषणं न कुर्यात्' —i.e., one though well versed in the scriptures should not search independently after the knowledge of Brahman. Cf. 'आचार्यवान् पुरुषो वेद'—a man who has accepted a teacher attains true knowledge. (Ch.6.14.2.)

3 *Humility etc.* : The reference is to the twenty virtues enumerated in the Gītā, Chapt. 13—verses 7 to 11. Cf. Bṛ. 4.4.23.

4 *Service etc.* : Cf. Gītā 4.34—'तद्विद्धि प्रणिपातेन परिप्रश्नेन सेवया'—'Know That, by prostrating thyself, by questions and by service. The wise who have realized the Truth will instruct thee in that Knowledge.'

The disciple must be well-equipped with all these qualifications and then the teacher, too, should instruct such a disciple properly. Bhagavān Śrī Śaṅkarācārya says in his commentary on Mu. 1.2.13.—'आचार्यस्याप्ययं नियमो यन्न्यायप्राप्तसच्छिष्यनिस्तारणमविद्यामहोदधेः'—On the part of the teacher, too, it is obligatory that he should instruct a disciple properly equipped with all the virtues as enumerated in the scriptures, and thus help him to cross the ocean of ignorance. Cf. Up. Sāh. 324. 16. 72. Śv. 6.23.

64. After having learnt the true purport of this book under the guidance of efficient and realized teachers one should devote one's life and soul to the practice of the grand theme, dealt with herein :

इमां विद्यां प्रयत्नेन योगी संध्यासु सर्वदा ।
समभ्यसेदिहामुत्रभोगानासक्तधीः सुधीः ॥६४॥

योगी One striving earnestly for union with the Supreme, सुधीः possessing excellent understanding, and इह-अमुत्र-भोग-अनासक्त-धीः detachment from pleasures here and hereafter, समभ्यसेत् must practise thoroughly, इमां this, विद्यां science, प्रयत्नेन with determined effort, संध्यासु during twilights, सर्वदा all his life.

One striving earnestly for union with the Supreme, possessing[1] excellence of understanding, and detachment[2] from pleasures of both earthly and heavenly character, must practise this science thoroughly and with determined efforts[3] during twilights,[4] all his life.[5]

1 *Possessing etc., : i.e.,* One who has done hearing (श्रवणम्) and reasoning (मननम्) for a considerable length of time and has thus qualified himself for contemplation (निदिध्यासनम्) on the Ātman.

2 *Detachment etc. :* See introduction to verse 1. The four fold means to the attainment of knowledge has been described there. Detachment means वैराग्यम् i.e., the renunciation of both the earthly and heavenly enjoyments. Cf. Panc. 6. 285.

3 *With determined efforts :* Cf.

लोकानुवर्तनं त्यक्त्वा त्यक्त्वा देहानुवर्तनम् ।
शास्त्रानुवर्तनं त्यक्त्वा स्वाध्यासापनयं कुरु ॥

Avoiding all social formalities, giving up the ideas of decorating the body, and abandoning too much studies of the scriputres, try, to totally remove the superimposition that has come upon you. Viv. Cu. 270.

4 *Twilights :* During twilights one should repeat, too, this treatise, with proper understanding.

5 *All his life* : Cf. 'स तु दीर्घकाल-नैरन्तर्य-सत्कारासेवितो दृढभूमिः'— It becomes firmly grounded by long, constant practice with great love (for the end to be attained). Yo. Sū. 1.14.

Success does not come in a day, but by long continued practice. Cf. Gītā, 18.52.

इति श्रीमत्सुरेश्वराचार्यविरचितं पञ्चीकरणवार्त्तिकं संपूर्णम् ।

Here ends the '*Vārttika*' composed by Śrī Sureśvarācārya on '*Pañcīkaraṇam*' of Bhagavān Śrī Śaṅkarācārya.

—o—

GLOSSARY

(*Figures indicate the numbers of Vārttika-ślokas*)

Abhimāna False identification (30, 34, 38, 43)
Abhyāsa Repeated practice (64)
Adhibhūta Sphere of the elements (12, 14-28)
Adhidaivika Sphere of the gods (12, 14-28)
Adhyātma Sphere of the body (12, 14-28)
Akṣarātmā The indestructible Spirit, *Iśvara* (44)
Amānitva etc. Virtues like humility etc. (63)
Anāsakti Detachment from enjoyments (64)
Anusandhāna Inquiry, Contemplation (34)
Ārūḍha-Bhāva Getting thoroughly established (56)
Ātmājñānam Ignorance pertaining to the Ātman (40)
Aum The sacred syllable 'AUM' is considered to be the nearest symbol of Brahman. Contemplating on 'Aum' according to the method prescribed in this book leads to realization, i.e., the knowledge of the unity of *Jīva* and Brahman. (1, 46-53)
Āvaraṇa The veiling power of Ignorance, which hides the real nature of the Self. (59)
Avidyā-Kāma-Karma Ignorance bringing desires and actions in its trail. (36)
Avyākṛta Same as *Ātmājñānam* (2, 40)
Avyakta Same as *Ātmājñānam* (2, 40)
Bhakti Devotion to God and Guru (53, 63)
Bhagavattama One firmly established in God-Consciousness (63)
Caitanyābhāsa Ignorance bears the reflection of the self-luminous Pure Consciousness in it. This reflection

or *Caitanyābhāsa* is what is called *Iśvara* in Vedānta (39)
(The Intellect, too, catches the reflection of the same self-luminous Pure Consciousness, thereby acquiring the property of Consciousness in itself. That reflection, *Caitanyābhāsa*, also known as *Bodhābhāsa* or *Cidābhāsa*, is what is known as *Jīva* in Vedānta.

Diṅ-Moha-Indu-Vibhāga The common wrong knowledge of mistaken directions and the manifoldness of the moon (58)

Sthūla Bhūta The subtle rudimentary five elements become gross only after undergoing the process of '*Pañcīkaraṇa*', i.e., five-fold combination. The gross elements go into the formation of the universe (7)

Guṇas Three in number—*Sattva*, *Rajas* and *Tamas*. These constitute the Māyā, the Primeval Energy, the cause of all illusions (2)

Heya Anything to be shunned (62)

Hiraṇya-garbha The Subtle objective-totality. See *Sūtra* (6, 39)

Iśvara The great cause of the universe, the Pure Consciousness associated with its own power Māyā (2, 43, 44)

Kāraṇa-Śarīra Causal body, i.e., Ignorance which brings about the entire creation (42)

Kośas Five in number, viz, *Annamaya Kośa*, *Prāṇamaya Kośa*, *Manomaya Kośa*, *Vijñānamaya Kośa*, and *Ānandamaya Kośa*. The first one, i.e., the *Annamaya Kośa* comprises the gross body and the next three constitute the subtle body while the last one, i.e., the *Ānandamaya Kośa* is what is known as the causal body. These are called *Kośas* (sheaths) being coverings over the Ātman

Kṛta-Kṛtya A state of perfection where nothing more achievable or knowable is left behind (56)

Liṅga Subtle body (36)

Māyā The inscrutable power of Brahman (2)

Mukta, Jīvan-Mukta and *Videha-Mukta*.
One who has attained liberation even while living is called a '*Jīvan-mukta*', and after the disintegration of the body the very same person is known as *Videha-mukta*, i.e., one having achieved 'Disembodied liberation' (56)

Pañcīkaraṇa The fivefold combination which the five subtle rudimentary elements have to undergo to become gross ones (8-10)

Paramānanda-Sandoha Literally it means a mass of Bliss. i.e., Bliss Infinite, or the state of final Beatitude (51)

Prājña The Consciousness, associated with the deep-sleep state and the causal body or Ignorance (43)

Prāṇa The vital force (five-fold) (35)

Prārabdha The actions of past lives which have given birth to the present body and have begun to produce results (58, 59)

Pratyagātmā The Innermost Self (37)

Puryaṣṭakam The eight cities. These together form the subtle body (36)

Sākṣī The Witness, the Innermost Self. All things are superimposed on It, which is actionless. It illumines everything and this illumining is called 'Knowing'. *Pratyagātmā, Antarātmā, Sākṣī, Kūṭastha*, all these mean the same Innermost Self (51)

Samādhi A state where the mind gets completely merged

in Consciousness, the Supreme Spirit (48,

Saṅkalpa The reflections of the mind (33)

Sammoha Confusion, Illusion, Ignorance (44)

Sandhyā Morning and evening twilights—suitable times for spiritual practice (64)

Śraddhā Unshakable faith in the teachings of Vedānta and one's own Guru (53)

Sthūla-Śarīra The gross body (11)

States (three) The waking, dream, and deep-sleep states (13, 29, 38, 42)

Sūkṣma Śarīra The subtle body (37)

Sūtra (*Sūtrātmā* or *Hiraṇyagarbha*) The subtle objective-totality (6)

Taijasa The Consciousness associated with the dream state and the subtle body (38)

Tanmātra Five fine elements (3)

Upādeya Something acceptable (62)

Vairāgya ("*Ihāmutra-phala-bhoga-virāga*") Renouncing all enjoyments here and hereafter (64)

Vaiṣṇavam Padam The status of Viṣṇu, the all-pervading Supreme Brahman (62)

Vāsudeva The all-pervading Supreme Spirit (51)

Vidyā Right knowledge, or the science which leads to Right knowledge (64)

Vikṣepa-Śakti The projecting power of Ignorance, which brings about the illusion of name and form (59)

Virāṭ The Consciousness associated with the aggregate of all gross bodies (7, 11)

Viśva The Consciousness which identifies itself with the individual gross body and the waking state (30)

Yogī One who strives hard for the knowledge of the unity of the individual soul with the Universal One (64)

VĀRTTIKA ŚLOKA INDEX